A Higher Calling:

A Biblical Guide for First Responders, Military, and Veterans

John Benjamin Jones

FOREWORD BY
LT. COL. DAVE GROSSMAN

Contents

A Higher Calling: A Biblical Guide for First Responders, Military, and Veterans

ISBN-13: (softcover) 9798869379863

ISBN-13: (e-book) 9798869379870

This book would not have come to fruition without the unconditional support of my beautiful wife, Emily, and our six amazing children.

Acknowledgments

I would like to take this opportunity to thank every first responder, member of the military, and veteran who was gracious enough to tell their stories and allow me to share them with you. Your courage, commitment, and faith are an inspiration to us all. As you will see, I have kept these individuals anonymous when possible. I would also like to express my most sincere thanks to you, the reader. I truly appreciate you taking the time to explore these topics in greater depth with me. I am humbled. Thank you.

Foreword

You hold in your hands one of the most important books of our age. The author's amazing selection of powerful personal narratives to bring this essential subject alive, combined with his masterful weaving together of all these threads into Scriptural concepts, has resulted in this "Biblical Guide to First Responders," which is to its realm what my books *On Killing* and *On Combat* have been in their fields.

The integration of authoritative quotes has been one of the ingredients that have helped to make my writing successful, and with John Jones and his *A Higher Calling*, my personal literary endeavors have met their match.

Consider just one powerful personal narrative in this book, from an individual overwhelmed by the devastation of a natural disaster and calling out to God in prayer:

> *His answer was not long in coming. He did*
> *not speak audibly, but He couldn't have*
> *been more clear if He had spoken to me*
> *out of a burning bush. I was patrolling*

> *an area outside of the security checkpoint when I came across an elderly African-American woman who had found a broom somewhere and had taken the initiative to start sweeping out a clean spot in the sea of trash. No one told her to do it, she just knew that it needed to be done so she did it. In that instant, I knew that God was showing me that He was there, a light in the darkness, illustrated by this one woman's selfless act. It wasn't much, but it showed me that one person can make a difference and God is showing us the hope that's just beyond the veil that our human eyes can see. He's there in all of our tragedies and triumphs. He's there with us every day loving us and calling us to be His light in this present darkness.*

That quote makes the hair stand up on my head. As a fellow wordsmith, I am in awe of such "gems" embedded within this book. And there is a *wealth* of such literary treasure to be found in this mighty and virtuous volume.

Future generations will look back in awe upon our magnificent "sheepdogs," the first responders who rose to the challenge to defend our "flock" in this tragic, violent era, much as we think of the heroes and lawmen of the wild west. But the violence of those bygone days is mostly a Hollywood myth. The violence of today is very real.

In order to recognize the demands up on our first responders, to understand how very much these magnificent men and women need the information in this book, to fully grasp what they face every day in answering this *Higher Calling*, you must first understand some critical concepts. When we look deeper, we will see that the situation is much, much worse than it looks.

Medical Technology is Holding Down the Murder Rate

The annual increase in homicides is a key factor in assessing the degree of violence in our society. The "number of dead people" is the measurement by which we judge the problem.

However, there is a major flaw in this measurement. We must understand that *the murder rate under-represents the level of violence*, because *medical technology is saving ever more lives.*

In 2002, Anthony Harris and a team of scholars from the University of Massachusetts and Harvard, published their landmark research in the journal *Homicide Studies.* They concluded that advances in medical technology between 1960 and 1999, *cut the murder rate to a third, or a quarter, of what it would otherwise be.* And the leaps and bounds of life-saving technology in the decades since then, has had a similar impact in saving the lives of even more victims of violence. Thus "preventing" ever more murders.

Therefore, you must multiply homicides in the 1990s by a factor of about 3.5 to compare with the 1960s. And a similar dynamic is in play between the 1990s and the 2020s.

Everyone understands the concept of "inflation adjusted dollars." When we finally start reporting "medically adjusted murders" then we will begin to appreciate just how desperately, tragically *bad* the situation has become. For every murder we report, *there are ever-increasing numbers of our citizens* physically maimed and scarred, and emotionally crippled and traumatized by violence. These are crimes that don't cross the threshold to become murder, because medical technology saved the victim's life.

Some medical experts believe that tourniquets alone may have cut the murder rate in half in just the last decade. Today almost all first responders (and many civilians) carry tourniquets, while twenty years ago this was unheard of. If a cop slaps on a tourniquet and saves a crime victim's life, they have prevented a murder.

And that is just one small aspect of the astounding medical technology being applied every day, holding down the body count and save lives. But also concealing just how violent and destructive our society has become.

(There is a temptation to use the "aggravated assault" data instead of murder data, but it is too easy to "fudge the figures" on "ag assault." Any seasoned old cop will tell you that we can make the ag assault rate say whatever you want it to say, by shifting that "magic line" between ag assault and "simple assault," very much like "grade inflation" in our schools. Murder is good data. Dead is dead, and it is hard to "fudge" those numbers. But to use murder rates over any period of time, we must allow for medical technology, just like allowing for inflation when comparing minimum wages across time.)

The annual increase in homicides in 2020 was over 30%. The worst we have ever seen previously is a 12% annual increase in the 1960s. But that comparison between 2020 and the 1960s completely breaks down! You must multiply homicides today by a factor of four, five, six, or seven (and maybe more) to compare with the 60s! What happened in 2020 is *10 to 20 times worse than anything we have ever seen before, and 2021 was even worse, up another 4%.*

Thus, you might already think that our first responders need spiritual help and guidance in their *Higher Calling* amidst the dangerous, violent world out there. But today, that need is demonstrably, irrefutably, "orders of magnitude" greater than you thought!

THE PSYCHOLOGICAL TRAUMA OF VIOLENCE

There is another important dynamic that we must consider. A monstrous mass murder by a single individual, can create more psychosocial trauma than countless deaths by disease. In its section on PTSD, the *DSM-5* (the "bible" of psychology and psychiatry) tells us that, whenever the cause of trauma is "human in nature" (such as assault, torture, or rape) the degree of trauma is usually "more severe and long lasting."

Millions die from disease every day, and it has little impact on our behavior. But one serial killer or serial rapist can paralyze a city. And one horrendous mass murder can stun a nation.

On 9-11, terrorists murdered 3,000 of our citizens. Our stock market crashed, our way of life changed, and we invaded two nations. That same your over 30,000 Americans died in traffic accidents, and nothing changed, *because they were accidents.*

I often say to my audiences, "You, tell me. Is there a difference between a tornado hitting your house and putting your family in the hospital, and criminals breaking into your house and beating your family into a hospital stay?" Most people would say there is all the difference in the world.

The magnitude of the problem is not recognized, because we do not take medical technology into account when we assess the "body count." Our nation (and our whole civilization, worldwide, because this effect is very much global in nature) is like a body suffering horrendous trauma, but the pain receptors are turned off! The trauma is still there, and the breakdown of the "body" is still happening.

Again, to whatever degree you were concerned about the impact of violence upon you, your loved ones, and society in general; today that concern should be amplified and focused, with an understanding of the psychologically corrosive and destructive impact of a violent incident.

Thus, the over-all societal harm of violent crime can be far greater than the harm caused by disease or other deaths by "natural causes." And *this* is the toxic, corrosive, psychologically destructive *sewer* that we ask our responders to work in, as they fulfill their *Higher Calling* every day.

WE ARE GETTING GOOD AT STOPPING THESE CRIMES!

Additionally, you must understand that our society in general, and our law enforcement community in particular, have become very good at stopping many horrific mass murders, before they even occur. I believe that today the Littleton Colorado school killers would have been caught before they committed their massacre in Columbine High School.

Across America, as I train law enforcement and school safety professionals, I hear a consistent message: "You never hear about the ones we stop." In schools and workplaces, we are no longer in denial (with some notable, tragic exceptions), and often take effective action before the crime occurs.

We are getting better at spotting and stopping these killers ahead of time. And when attempted mass murders do occur, rapid and effective response by our first responders (police and emergency medical personnel) are saving lives and holding down the body-count.

Yet still homicide rates are exploding. And the number of attacks is also increasing.

The National Center for Education Statistics, "2021 Violent Deaths at School" report (Table 3), tells us that after a modern low of 11 reported "school shootings" in the 2009-10 school year (roughly half of these incidents each year are with "injuries only" while the rest are "shootings with deaths"), it went up as follows:

17 in 2010-11
14 in 2011-12
22 in 2012-13
37 in 2013-14
35 in 2014-15
27 in 2015-16
38 in 2016-17
59 in 2017-18
78 in 2018-19
77 in 2019-20
93 in 2020-21

The final two years are particularly troubling because schools were closed for a large portion of those years, due to the pandemic.

THIS IS NOT NORMAL, IT IS NOT "BUSINESS AS USUAL"

Next, we must understand that *this is not normal.* Mass murders and vicious massacres (like those we hear about almost every day in the news) are comparatively rare in previous criminal history. There have always have been mass murders. (Often motivated by war, religious or tribal conflict, or ideology.) But they are fairly rare, and the "lone wolf" massacres like we are seeing today are profoundly rare in ages past. Now they are everywhere.

In my own research I have tracked *mass-murders* committed by *juveniles,* in their *schools.* Such an event is unprecedented in human history, until very recently. Here is a list of *school massacres* committed by *juveniles* (up through 2014), from my book *Assassination Generation:*

-1975: 2 murdered in Brampton, Canada (The very first that I can find in human history.)

-1979: 2 murdered in San Diego, California

-1985: 2 murdered in Spanaway, Washington

-1989: 2 murdered in Rauma, Finland

-1993: 2 murdered in Grayson, Kentucky

-1995: 2 murdered in Lynnville, Tennessee

-1996: 3 murdered in Moses Lake, Washington

-1997: 2 murdered in Bethel, Alaska

-1997: 2 murdered in Pearl, Mississippi (the killer also murdered his mother)

-1997: 3 murdered (and 5 wounded) in Paducah, Kentucky

-1998: 5 murdered (and 10 wounded) in Jonesboro, Arkansas

-1998: 2 murdered (and 25 wounded) in Springfield, Oregon

-1999: 13 murdered (and 21 wounded) in Littleton, Colorado

-2003: 2 murdered (and 4 wounded) in Nakhon, Thailand

-2004: 4 murdered (and 5 wounded) in Carmen, Argentina

-2005: 7 murdered (and 5 wounded) in Red Lake, Minnesota (the killer also murdered his grandparents)

-2009: 15 murdered (and 9 wounded) in Winnenden, Germany

-2012: 3 murdered (and 3 wounded) in Chardon, Ohio

-2013: 2 murdered (and 7 injured) in La Loche, Canada (the killer -also murdered two cousins at a home.)

-2014: 4 murdered (and 3 wounded) in Marysville, Washington

-2014: 2 murdered (and 1 wounded) in Moscow, Russia

(None of these totals includes the killers when they commit suicide)

Also, in 2002, a 19-year-old, expelled high school student murdered 16 people at his former school in Erfurt, Germany, and an 18-year-old student murdered nine in his school in Tuusula, Finland, in 2007. Because these killers were over the age of 18, however, they don't qualify for the "juvenile mass-murder hit parade."

Note that some of the crimes in the list above occurred in Argentina, Canada, Finland, Germany, Russia and Thailand. The first was in Canada, and a 17-year-old student in Germany set the *all-time record juvenile mass murders in human history* (not just in a school, but anywhere), a "record" that holds to this very day. The two

Columbine killers murdered 13 people between them, but the killer in Germany gunned down 15 by himself.

Such crimes have never happened before in human history. Today, massacres and the threat of such crimes are a reality in nearly every nation. *Five thousand years of human history, 500 years of gunpowder weapons, and 150 years of repeating firearms, and not once did any juvenile commit such a crime in their school, until 1975. Now these crimes are a worldwide phenomenon.*

Meanwhile, if we zoom out and look worldwide, we see that in 2018 in Russia, 20 were murdered and 70 wounded by an 18-year-old perpetrator on a college campus. In China we see a series of knife massacres across the years, with horrendous body counts, in schools, kindergartens, and even nurseries.

Thus, this book and its essential ministry to those who follow *A Higher Calling*, are not just vital information for America. Around the world people are asking the question: How can we possibly deal with these violent times?

This breakdown of law and order, the systematic erosion of the fabric of our civilization, is the single most important issue facing us today. And the most horrific part is that most people don't even know what is happening!

But our first responders? Those who go in harm's way every day? They know it, they *feel* it. And the tragic survivors of this virus of violence? The ever-greater numbers whose lives have been preserved by medical marvels? And the loved ones of those slaughtered in the midst of this cancer of crime? They know. Oh, they know. And they all cry out to God, in terrible anguish and suffering.

(And if we think like a detective, if we think like a scientist, we will ask the question: "What has changed?

What is the *new* factor worldwide?" The answer to that question can be found in my books, *Assassination Generation* and *On Killing; The Price and Process of Learning to Kill*.)

GOD'S ANSWER

And God hears every cry for help. God even hears that faint prayer of despair, whispered under your breath. In her song "Rescue" Lauren Daigle says, "He hears our every SOS. Oh yes, oh yes."

Let there be no doubt, God loves us with a love that is "to infinity and beyond" any love we can imagine. God loves us so much, that when we weep, He tastes the salt.

I tell all my military and first responder audiences that this is an existential question that every human being asks. You see terrible things every day, and you can't help but ask: "How could a loving God allow such terrible things to happen?" The problem is, you think you know the answer based on Hollywood and TV. And if you consider for just a moment, you will recognize that just about everything *they* tell us is wrong.

We. Are. Not. God's puppets. A loving Father would not be a "helicopter parent" hovering over you for a lifetime, manipulating every moment of every day to protect you. God *does* hear our prayers, we *should* hold everything up to Him in prayer, and he *does* answer prayers. You may have heard it said, "If you love something, let it go. If it comes back, it is really yours." *That* is how much God loves us.

God loves us enough to let everyone make their own decisions. That means a lot of people make bad decisions, and a lot of very bad things happen.

You say, "God, why don't you do something?!"
He says, "I did. I sent you."
I say in my book *On Spiritual Combat*,

Please don't curse God when your prayers are not answered the way you think they should be.

In the end, we will all die. God's greatest achievement is not to give us wealth or comfort or a few more days in this fallen world. God's greatest gift, his most awesome, miraculous achievement, is to save our souls and to pay the price for our sin with the blood of Jesus so that we can be adopted children in his family for eternity. And the most important thing we can ever pray for is not that our loved ones will live a little longer, not that they will have comfort or ease in this world. The greatest thing we can pray for, work for, and strive for is that they will come to the knowledge of God's salvation and embrace it as their own.

Again, as I tell my audiences, if you have a remote idea that there might be a life after death, then you must recognize that it is the most important thing in the universe. So remember, everybody dies. Eventually every nation will fall. In the end, our sun will die. But eternity continues.

Keep your eye on the big picture. Don't let the things of this world pull you down.

Jesus said, "Greater love has no one than this: that they *give* their lives for their friends" (John 15:13). To which I would add: there are many ways to *give* your life. Sometimes the greatest love is not to sacrifice your life, but to live a life of sacrifice. And *that* is what our first responders do, every day, as they answer *A Higher Calling*!

Looking again at John 15:13, it is worth noting that

many people *will* die for their friends. Audie Murphy was the most decorated American Soldier in World War II. When asked why he did it, his answer was, "They were killing my friends."

Yes, a lot of people will die for their friends. But what kind of person will die for strangers? What manner of love is this: that they will go out the door every day, going in harm's way, and putting their life on the line *for people they don't even know*?

The opposite of evil is not good. The opposite of evil is *love*, because evil is the absence of love. Love defeats evil, as light banishes the darkness. And our first responders truly embody the sacrificial love that Jesus was talking about in John 15:13.

That is how much God loves us. He loves us enough to send those first responders to be there in your hour of greatest need. And. This. Is. Truly *A Higher Calling*!

Most of all, the greatest love and the greatest achievement is that, "God ... sent His only begotten son to die for us, that whoever believes on Him shall not perish, but shall have everlasting life" (John 3:16).

FOR SUCH A TIME AS THIS

Thus, you see what our first responders must face, every day, in these tragic times. And thus, you see how very badly they need God and His amazing Grace to uplift, empower, and sustain them in their magnificent *Higher Calling*.

That is why this book is so very important. It is about equipping our first responders, and all those who support them, to engage is virtuous, successful, spiritual warfare. In normal war we win, in large part, by killing the enemy. In spiritual warfare, we win by *saving* people! Saving them physically, and most of all (so *infinitely* more important) saving them spiritually.

Thus, this book and the endeavors of those who read and apply it, represents the most important thing in the universe: souls saved for *eternity*.

And so dear brothers and sisters, with all my heart I encourage you, I *exhort* you to read, study, and apply this book. Not just first responders and those who support them, but *everyone*. Because. We. Are. All! Soldiers on the battlefield of souls!

Study this book. Apply this book. Buy copies and give them to your friends and all your local first responders. So that they too may boldly walk the path of *A Higher Calling*!

Lt. Col. Dave Grossman (US Army, ret.)
Author of *On Killing, On Combat, On Spiritual Combat, On Spiritual Warfare, Bulletproof Marriage,* and *Assassination Generation*
Director, Grossman On Truth
www.GrossmanOnTruth.com

Introduction

Over the years as I have grown in my Christian walk, I have studied the life stories of some of the most notable theological minds from the last century. Some stories are of Christian men and women who overcame extreme hardships and suffering. Many of these stories' central theme was how their faith brought on or directly increased the suffering of these individuals. C.S. Lewis, Bonhoeffer, Corrie Ten Boom, and others endured extreme circumstances. None were ever the same. Some did not survive.

More recently, books penned by or about Christian members of the military who have overcome extreme situations have become wildly popular. Books by or about Lieutenant General Boykin, Chad Williams, and Adam Brown have shed light on the struggles that Christians within the military face in and out of combat. '*Fearless, The Adam Brown Story*' is one book I highly recommend.

As amazing and inspirational as these stories are, they are books about an individual overcoming a specific or set of trials, how their faith sustained them during these difficult times, and ultimately how they were able to come out on the other side a better person. As the title of the recent book by Lt Col. Dave Grossman and Adam Davis implies, 'On Spiritual Combat' comes close to what I have been searching for. I have yet to find a book that talks directly about some of the common issues faced by Christian police officers, firefighters, emergency medical providers, and those serving in the military. I have interviewed dozens of Christians from every conceivable level of first responder capacity.

This includes members from federal agencies, state, local, and county police departments, big city and rural firefighters, dispatchers, nurses, paramedics, and emergency medical technicians. And I would be remiss if I did not mention the members of each branch of the United States military, many of whom have served in medical and combat capacities.

I had three distinct purposes in mind while writing this book. The first is to show that God is sovereign and worthy of all honor, glory, and praise, even during the traumatic events faced by first responders, military, and veterans. The second purpose is for this book to be a quick access guide for those of us serving in some form of first responder capacity. Thirdly, I want this book to be a source of encouragement for you.

The driving force behind this book is to remind you that you are not alone. And this reminder is not just for those uneventful hours when nothing seems to be happening but also when fear reaches inside you, and those icy hands knead your guts like dough. That's when I want you to know in your soul that you are not alone.

How does one give advice to Christian first responders? What qualifies someone to attempt such a thing? Does it take a Ph.D. in Theology from one of the country's best seminaries? C.S. Lewis had a Ph.D. in English and was an academic lecturer. While well-educated, does the fact that he was not a seminary-trained pastor undermine his scriptural prowess? After all, he is widely considered one of the most astute theological minds of the twentieth century.

What about a full-time Pastor who volunteers as an agency chaplain?

Corrie Ten Boom was the first woman in Holland to be licensed as a watchmaker.

Did this mean that she was disqualified from ministering to hundreds of fellow female prisoners during her internment in a World War II Nazi concentration camp? Does someone with formal religious and counseling training who assists first responders as close to immediately as possible after a traumatic incident meet the criteria you have set forth in your mind as someone qualified to provide guidance and advice to first responders? While this may be a more accurate description of what many would imagine meets the requirements to which most first responders would agree, I believe the qualities that make for a qualified advisor to Christian first responders is any person who:

1. Is a Christian,
2. Is an experienced first responder,
3. Is willing to put themselves on the line to help their fellow first responders.

At the time of this writing, I have nearly three decades of continuous experience in the first responder field. This experience has been earned through hard lessons from combat roles within the military, international missions work, local-level law enforcement, emergency medical work, and significant time as a Federal Agent. I have been in the muck and mire, both physically and spiritually. I have stared into that dark abyss and have been snatched back by God's gentle hand. This is in no way intended to suggest that my experiences have been more intense than others. Nor is it my intention to dismiss the experiences of the countless military, veteran, and first responders who have gone through trials far greater than mine.

This book will look at some ways Christians can do the hard job required of them and still be a light unto the world. Together, we will walk through such things as how to approach relationships, both personal and professional, what it looks like to train your body and mind to endure the assaults you will face, violence, death, loss, and trauma, and how to continue to make an impact after you are done in your official first responder capacity. The common theme you will see throughout this book is mindset.

This book is written in an easy style, or at least that was my intention. I have attempted to use a casual voice, with as few acronyms and jargon as possible. It is my hope that my writing style, anecdotes, or observations do not come across as offensive, demeaning, or simplistic. Any grammatical errors, poor syntax, or flow are completely and solely the responsibility of the author. Unless noted otherwise, all scripture quotes are sourced from the New International Version Bible.

CHAPTER ONE
TRAINING

> "Do you not know that in a race all the
> runners run, but only one gets the
> prize? Run in such a way as to get the
> prize."
>
> — 1 CORINTHIANS 9:24

I t should come as no surprise to you that there is an inherently physical aspect of the first responder profession. It's also no surprise that your profession is reactionary by nature. Because of this necessarily reactionary role, it's no wonder many first responders cannot carve out time for physical fitness during work hours. This is especially true for law enforcement officers, emergency medical technicians/paramedics, and hospital-based emergency medical providers. Unfortunately, most agencies fail to recognize that physical training and its upkeep are as important as the other perishable skill sets required by your profession.

Similar to how every single first responder agency

mandates recurrent training for the continual proficiency of firearms, handcuffing, CPR, spinal stabilization, and a host of other perishable skills on a regular basis to mitigate liability and agency culpability, so too should this emphasis be placed on physical fitness. An agency misses a vital aspect of employee development when they do not maximize physical fitness development.

Several studies over the last few decades have proven the benefits of even moderate physical activity, such as walking at a moderate pace for just thirty minutes. The results are holistic, meaning they are not just physical in nature. Some of these benefits manifest as increased bone density and improved cholesterol and blood pressure. A noticeable increase in mental function and physical stamina are also common results from a moderate increase in your exercise routine. These benefits affect the employee in every aspect of their life, not just on the job. So, let's look at how each of these plays in your favor.

> Everyone who competes in the games goes into strict training. They do it to get a crown that will not last, but we do it to get a crown that will last forever. 26. Therefore, I do not run like someone running aimlessly; I do not fight like a boxer beating the air. 27. No, I strike a blow to my body and make it my slave so that after I have preached to others, I myself will not be disqualified for the prize."
>
> — 1 CORINTHIANS 25-27

Increased bone density reduces the risk of injury during physical assault and arrest situations. This reduces tissue, tendon, and ligament damage during load-bearing stresses, such as running or chasing a suspect. Every first responder has load-bearing activity throughout the majority of their workday.

Cardio Care

There is a reason that so many first responders suffer from fatal heart attacks. I have been in this field for a long time, and, unfortunately, I have heard more than a few first responders say that they are not interested in improving their cardiac health. Every time I hear a colleague speaking this way, I am saddened. I am saddened, not just because I started my career in the military medical services, but because statements like this indicate a lackadaisical mentality that puts the first responder (and, by proximity, their partners) in greater danger.

This outlook stems from the unrealistic belief that nothing 'really bad' will happen to them directly. Simply increasing good cholesterol, decreasing bad cholesterol, and lowering blood pressure mitigate the potential for plaque buildup, stroke, and cardiac arrest. This also helps the first responder deal more effectively with the physical and emotional stress associated with this work.

We are victims of shift work and, as a profession, have a notorious reputation for persistent sleep deprivation. Increasing physical activity by thirty minutes has been shown to improve sleep, sleep quality, and depression. It has been linked to reduced anxiety and increased mood.

It has been said that age is not the deciding factor in

energy loss; it is inactivity. We all remember how virile we felt when first entering the first responder field. We were ready to take on the world. We were going to fix all the woes in our community. Remember how you felt halfway through your academy? I will go out on a limb here, take a wild guess, and say you were exhausted. You dragged yourself into class in the morning with coffee, Red Bull, or some other energy drink (maybe all three) coursing through your veins, fighting that uphill battle to help you slog through the day. I would argue this was a result of poor sleep.

As the academy progressed, there were ever-increasing demands on your time and harder tests for which you had to study. It was like trying to drink from a firehose with more information coming at you faster than you thought possible. And because there are only 24 hours in a day, sleep was one of the first things that had to adjust. What about all you military folk? How did you feel four months into your year-long deployment?

You were probably doing everything we did in our academy while throwing down a few cans of RipIt for good measure. Fast forward to present day, where there are daunting caseloads, unending court appearances, work and home chores, familial commitments, church commitments, and so many other things vying for your limited time. Through all of this, you must now prioritize getting back into shape.

SKILLS THAT PERISH

In the same way, our physical fitness may be lacking, we must recognize that formal martial training is woefully lacking in many departments. There is a basic level of training in the academy. This training is generally comprehensive enough to get one proficient in effecting an arrest. Unfortunately, this training comes with little follow-up training, if any. I have had law enforcement officers tell me their department does not train in arrest techniques because the officers perform arrests so often during their normal work functions that they consider it on-the-job training!

Training in a martial skill is a must for all first responders. For law enforcement, restraint training is a perishable skill. How many times have non-law enforcement first responders been forced to restrain a violent, unruly, or dangerous patient? This situation usually results from a kinetic encounter before law enforcement is on the scene.

I have a fairly extensive fighting background, which includes wrestling, Jiu-Jitsu, and Filipino stick and knife training. It is not my intention to debate the merits of any one particular martial arts system over another. Nor is it intended to get into a detailed listing of the pros and cons of the various systems of martial arts training.

While the grappling arts like Jiujitsu, Wrestling, and Sambo are popular amongst firefighters, law enforcement officers, and corrections officers, they are equally beneficial to medics, nurses, military service members, and veterans. Boxing (the sweet science) is still a highly effective martial discipline useful for any first responder, regardless of their specific field. As is Thai boxing (A.K.A. Muay Thai or Kickboxing), Eskrima, Judo, or any other traditional martial arts.

The only argument I will make regarding selecting a martial art is this: The best martial arts training is the one you attend. It is useless for you to sign up for a Jiu-Jitsu class if you never show up. Committing to improving your martial arts skills has the added benefit of increasing your physical fitness. Bonus! Two birds with one stone. Archilochus, the ancient Greek philosopher and writer, was correct when he said, *"We do not rise to the level of our expectations, we fall to the level of our training."* It is up to you to ensure that the level of training to which you fall is adequate to overcome the threat. Whatever form that may be.

Accountants, mechanics, secretaries, teachers, and pastors all benefit from physical fitness and martial arts training. How much more will this benefit you as a first responder? Physical fitness training inoculates you to the stressors of life. When you run hard, lift heavy weights, or otherwise push yourself, you make it easier for your body to deal with the incredible physiologic stresses encountered in the first responder profession.

Train for Victory in Battle

Competitive shooting events get you used to thinking, moving, and quickly assessing threat target identification in a loud, energetic, and slightly chaotic environment. You get the added benefit of shot placement recognition, rounds fired count, and 360-degree situational awareness. Making these split-second decisions on which targets to shoot in such a hectic environment directly relates to the highly confused reality of an officer-involved shooting situation.

Scenario-based training inoculates you to real-world situations that you may not generally experience in an average day but may encounter someday. These scenarios stretch your mind so that you can function if you are exposed to a similar situation. Often, people who first encounter bad situations respond by freezing up.

These individuals have never let their brains expand into the possibility of finding themselves in whatever bad situation happens. That 'Deer in the Headlights' look is their brain desperately trying to process the information, formulate a course of action, rejecting each in turn, and coming up short. Running these training scenarios also lets you make mistakes in a relatively safe environment where the risk of loss of life or limb is very low.

Training in the martial arts gives you the confidence to know that you can deal with physical altercations both on and off the job. This confidence allows you to go into highly stressful situations with a calm mind, thinking clearly about how to manage what is going on around you. You are a much more effective responder when you can efficiently process a chaotic scene.

I was a full-time training instructor in many agencies, companies, and military units throughout my career. One thing I have seen in each of these sectors is that there are motivated individuals ready and willing to bring their 'A-game' to the training venue. Unfortunately, there are also those individuals who do whatever they can in order to get out of scenario training. The person who avoids scenario training primarily has one of two motivators for doing so.

First motivator: This person is completely unsure of their abilities and does not want to look ridiculous in front of their peers, even though their refusal to train makes them look ridiculous in front of their peers. Second motivator: They are overly confident in their abilities. They are convinced that they are better than their peers and, therefore, do not need to train. Think about the consequences of either of these examples. If you slack off on your job requirements training, physical fitness, martial arts, or spiritual education, you are essentially saying that

you are already good enough. I hate to break it to you—
you're not.

Every Christian has been called to excellence. As Christian first responders, you have shown that you have what it takes to live by a high set of personal and professional standards, strong legal and ethical boundaries, and clear direction. You have dedicated your life to be marked by a quality of integrity, hard work, and discipline. You are not a stranger to participating in a rigorous training regime in order to achieve a specific goal. We have all done it, right? But what about developing a rigorous spiritual training regime?

> "For physical training is of some value, but
>   godliness has value for all things,
>   holding promise for both the present
>   life and the life to come."

> — 1 TIMOTHY 4:8

What does it look like to develop your spiritual muscles, and how do you run the race as a Christian first responder in such a way as to get an eternal award? There are two main areas that require strict spiritual training. These are simply your inward and your outward approach to spiritual training.

Some of the inward spiritual training practices involve things such as your worship, prayer life, and biblical study regime. Like we did for the physical aspects, let us dive deeper into each of these. The Oxford Dictionary defines worship as[1]:

Noun:

*1: reverence offered a divine being or supernatural
power
also: an act of expressing such reverence*

*2: a form of religious practice with its creed and
ritual*

*3: extravagant respect or admiration for or devotion
to an object of esteem
worship of the dollar*

Verb:
*1: to honor or show reverence for as a divine being or
supernatural power*

*2: to regard with great or extravagant respect, honor,
or devotion*

Nowhere does it say that worship is regulated by how loudly you sing at church, how animated you are while singing, or by only listening to worship music. Both the act and essence of worship are the reverence for a deity, in our case, Jesus Christ. Worship can be found in the small acts you perform that honor God–giving a stuffed animal to a child abuse victim, the quiet prayer for a coworker struggling with personal issues, or going out of your way to buy a meal for a homeless person in need. Any of these are examples of how a first responder might worship.

The Weapons of Our Warfare – Prayer

While prayer is certainly a form of worship, intentional prayer is a deeply personal worship between you and the

Lord. Intentional, or intercessory, prayer is exactly what it sounds like. Identifying specific people or situations and intentionally praying for a specific result. When you tell someone that you will pray for them, do you say a quick line or two in your head at the time you offer this prayer support? Even though this technically meets the requirements of praying for them, this type of superficialness has generally been regarded as fickle.

Or do you set aside a specific part of your dedicated prayer time to intentionally identify the person(s) and their situation? This is where many Christians believe the proverbial rubber meets the road in your transition into being an effective prayer warrior. Achieving this level of communication between you and God on behalf of another person makes the Devil literally shake with frustration. What about continuing to offer prayers with this level of intentionality regularly until they have passed through their personal storm? Do you voluntarily continue praying for them in their newfound calm?

Achieving this level is the Olympic Gold Medal standard of intentional prayer, but this does not absolve you from making progress. This is an area that every first responder can improve upon without carving out any extra time from their day. While having a specific 'War Room' in your home where you go to pray is a great idea, the reality is that you just may not have the time or space. What you do have is a continuous inner dialogue. You may only have time to offer a 'fickle' quick line or two while the situation is actively occurring. Focusing your thoughts on prayer throughout your day increases your worship and develops the personal relationship we all need with Jesus. An example of this comes from a Deputy Sheriff.

"I was the third Deputy Sheriff to respond to a motor vehicle accident involving a bus full of high school band students that went off a bridge and fell over 60 feet into a creek bed. Within minutes, first responders from nearly a dozen law enforcement agencies and fire departments arrived on scene. As you can imagine, it was quite chaotic.

There was an overwhelming feeling of helplessness. I prayed as I rushed down the embankment and plunged into the creek. I prayed as I transported kids and adult chaperones to the designated triage area. I prayed I performed CPR on a 14-year-old. I prayed for hours. I prayed for strength, guidance, and clarity of thought. I prayed for the kids who were not as physically harmed but would be forever scarred. I prayed for the boy I performed CPR on, and his mother who had chaperoned and now stood over my partner and me and wailed in anguish, and not just from her physical injuries.

The Lord granted me the ability to perform my duties that day. He also blessed the majority of passengers by sparing all but four. Our prayer may not be answered in the way we want, but I realize now that every prayer we say is answered the way God wants it to be."

— J.J. OMAHA, NE

Can you empathize with this deputy? Every single first responder has an example like this. As Christians, it is incumbent upon you to bring your struggles to the Lord. However, your situation does not need to be this extreme to be effective intercessory prayer. Regular prayer for your family, coworkers, and friends reaps tremendous dividends for both you and them.

STUDY TO SHOW YOURSELF APPROVED

Biblical study is the final inward spiritual training aspect we will look into. What books of the Bible are you working through? How many chapters do you read per week? What other spiritual books are mentoring you?

Reading scripture gives you the clarity of thought to discern between the schemes and attacks of the world so that your heart and spirit will be protected. When you fail to study scripture, you open yourself up to the lies that this world throws at you. These lies are not always blatant attempts to get you to sin.

Actually, those are the easier lies to defend against. It is the subtle shifting of your worldview away from a biblical one to a more secular one where the true danger lies. Generally speaking, this change in your worldview does not happen all at once but is a progressive erosion over months and years. Unfortunately, all too often, the voices trying to get you to compromise are from those with whom you serve and who wear a badge.

Biblical study is the *only* way to resist the massive onslaught of secular influences. Look to your kids as an example (or a niece or nephew if you do not have kids of your own). They are thrown to the wolves whenever they go to school, the mall, or a non-believing friend's house. Shoot, just turn on the television or watch YouTube ads closely, and you will see that the influence these kids face is tremendous. You voluntarily wage war with the darkness every time you start your shift. While they probably do not get exposed to the same level of influence as you daily, they do not have the same coping mechanisms you possess to deal with such influences.

If you claim to be a Christian first responder and do not

spend quality time in God's word, it is akin to enforcing felony laws without ever having gone through an academy *or* studying the statute elements of those laws. Can you imagine how well *that* would turn out? Get into scripture. Read daily. Show your children that biblical study is important. Then, you can be more than just a talking head when you encourage the kids in your life.

Ultimately, what you do every day by holding this razor-thin line between chaos and order is done to glorify God and point people to His saving grace, whether through overt evangelism or showing Christ's love through your demeanor and actions. You can wade into the fray with every intention of helping the people of your community, but Christ is the only way that these people will truly be saved from their situations. If you approach each shift with this in mind, it may change how you look at the people you encounter that day.

This was the inspiration for how this book came to be. Having gone through a variety of spiritual books, I noticed there were very few that specifically and accurately addressed the unique challenges Christian first responders face on a daily basis. This is not said to denigrate these books. All of them were beneficial in their own way. It is just that there is a particular set of burdens Christian first responders face that the rest of society cannot even begin to fathom.

Again, I am not going to place specific demands on which books of the bible you should read or in which order you should read them. Neither will I give you a specific number of chapters you should read daily or weekly. What I will say is: You must read your bible. Daily if feasible. And you should have at least one prayer session outside of mealtimes. Now, I know this sounds like this will take an inordinate amount of time, especially if there is currently no scripture reading or active prayer time (no judgment). I recommend starting small. There is a very popular program that follows the book of Proverbs.

There are seven months in the year with 31 days on the calendar, and there are 31 chapters in the book of Proverbs. Read one chapter daily and pray on the main point that speaks to you that day. It's as easy as that to develop the habit of prayerful biblical reading daily. I started out reading one chapter in Psalm and one chapter in Proverbs.

Starting with Genesis 1:1 and Matthew 1:1, I have expanded this daily to four chapters. At the time of this writing, I have now been able to read the bible in its entirety three times. The more disciplined you become in your mindset, the easier it will be to make the time to seek God through His word.

Improvements to your inward spiritual training will automatically manifest in improvements to your outward spiritual training. Your outward practice is expressed in several different ways, including, but not limited to your participation at church (not just attendance), your fellowship with other believers, and your evangelism and service to your community.

Participation at church is vital for a Christian. We will not get into the weeds regarding doctrine, but plugging yourself into a Bible-believing local church is essential for your spiritual training. The friendships, mentorship, and spiritual refreshing that occurs in the local church are true gifts from God. This is something we see as we read Proverbs 13:20, which says, *"Walk with the wise and become wise, for a companion of fools suffers harm,"* and Galatians 6:2, *"Carry each other's burdens, and in this way you will fulfill the law of Christ.*" This also holds true for small group participation.

Small groups are a micro expression of the church. Every aspect of church membership is hyper-focused when you commit to becoming a member of a small group. Romans 10:17 says, "*Consequently, faith comes from hearing the message, and the message is heard through the word about Christ,*" which is critical for the Christian first responder. I can hear the excuse now, "*I work mid-shift and can't join a small group,*" "*I have too many other commitments, and I'm not able to go to a small group every week,*" or my favorite, "*I am so physically exhausted when I get off work that I couldn't even think about going to a small group.*" While these are legitimate reasons for not being able to attend a small group occasionally, we must prioritize gathering in person with like-minded people.

I interviewed a group of Federal Air Marshals whose job is to travel the world and protect commercial civil aviation from terrorist attacks. The very nature of their job keeps these men and women away from home regularly. A few Christian Federal Air Marshals developed a small group through personal email.

They communicate with each other from every corner of the globe and encourage each other through the trials that come with being away from home for days and weeks at a time. There is no requirement that demands you be physically present in the small group. There are so many tools available that make it harder *not* to be involved with a small group. Apps, email, social media rooms, and church-sponsored online education are great ways to fellowship together at little to no cost. Experiment with some of the different systems and see what works for you and your small group.

Now is the time to develop your personal training plan. Just as you would design a workout regimen to lower your mile-and-a-half run time or increase your bench press in order to lift a certain weight, the same holds true for spiritual training. The goal is continual progression. Fortunately, because the goal is progression over perfection when it comes to spiritual training, time is on your side. Remember that you can use this to your advantage. With that said, we cannot use this as an excuse to delay our spiritual training.

We must not live aimless lives. Are you up to meeting the challenge which has been leveled? It is now up to you to work out your spiritual training plan—both inward and outward. Do not delay.

What would that look like if you asked yourself how to please God to the maximum in your position? What would be the result? What kind of reward would you receive? Would it change your perspective in how you approach work if you realized that the one handing out our awards is not your boss but God Himself?

Challenge Coin:

- Finding time in our busy schedules for spiritual work is a significant battle. Identify three separate time wasters in your life. How can you reclaim them? What spiritual activity can you replace them with?
- Develop an actionable plan. Make it easy for the first two weeks, then dial up the intensity as you gain momentum. The goal is to do something. If you're already doing something, then slowly start adding to it. No more wasting time in your spiritual life. You do not want to be like the boxer who only shadowboxes and trains. Remember, you are getting in the ring to fight whether you like it or not.
- Present your spiritual training plan to another first responder and ask them to hold you accountable with weekly progress checks, as well as to encourage you in your journey.

CHAPTER TWO
WORK RELATIONSHIPS

"You are the salt of the earth. But if the salt loses its saltiness how can it be made salty again? It is no longer good for anything except to be trampled underfoot."

— MATTHEW 5:13

As Christians, we refer to each other as '*Brother*' and '*Sister*.' This is done for a couple of different reasons. First, we are children of the most high God. While we have different mothers, we all have the same Father (as the saying goes). Secondly, the New Testament apostles regularly refer to the believers in the local congregations as *Adelphoi*, Greek for siblings or familial connection, or a blood relative. This same strong familial connection holds true for first responders, military, and veterans.

The reasoning behind this connection is utterly different, though. First responders and military identification as brothers and sisters are borne from the common cause they face. They are united through their shared experiences, hardships, and suffering. This unity and bond hold true for veterans from different eras. While the experience of a combat veteran of Afghanistan is wholly different than that of a combat veteran from Vietnam, they will, nevertheless, share a bond that non-combat persons can never grasp, even when that non-combat person is an actual blood sibling. Retired and active first responders can connect with each other even if they have never walked the same streets or dealt with the same people.

It should then be understood that it is a deeply personal matter when someone from the first responder, military, or veteran community refers to you as '*brother*' or '*sister*.' It is not an accidental or flippant connotation. The use of this term is completely conscious and deliberate. How much more endearing is this to you when used between believers within these professions?

This 'Brotherhood' or 'Sisterhood' can be harnessed to make you a more effective Christian first responder. By the very nature of this career field, you will be drawn into relationships with people who share similar experiences. This is natural. How much better for you, your family, and your walk with Christ if you seek out other Christians within your field to have these working relationships? While these relationships will mitigate your struggles, they will not eliminate them.

Beyond Reproach

Regardless of any preconceived expectations you may have of your non-first responder brothers and sisters from church or the seemingly endless barrage of Insta-perfect posts being plastered all over social media, it is difficult to maintain a vibrant walk with Christ. It can be an extremely complex issue as well. Some of you may say, "*What's so complex? Just live like Jesus, and everything will end up alright.*" If this sounds like you, let me be the first to congratulate you.

While this is a completely true statement, you can stop reading here, for there will be nothing new you can learn from this book that you do not already know. The reality of this statement is how many of us are able to live this daily through all the bad things to which we are exposed, the horrors we experience, and the trauma we cannot unsee. There are complexities that come with our profession.

The majority of first responders I have talked with tell stories of how they have changed from their naïve early first years on the job into a hardened and jaded person. Every single one of these people claims that, at some point during their career, they have become less idealistic, more cynical or angry, and generally less caring towards people, whether on the job or off-duty. As each of you can attest, this job has directly impacted your professional and personal relationships. And all too often, this impact has not been for the better.

The last chapter discussed the need for and offered suggestions to improve physical and spiritual fitness. You need the stamina these techniques will build to help you deal with the selfishness, poor decisions, and pure evil you experience daily. Continued exposure to this evil is one of the leading causes taking a toll on your spirit. But how wonderful that you have the God of the universe to fall upon! Not one of your unsaved coworkers has this escape. Think about that for a second. This is why it is so important for you to refresh your spirit.

"Humble yourselves, therefore, under
God's mighty hand, that he might lift
you up in due time. 7. Cast all your
anxiety on him because he cares for
you."

— 1 Peter 5: 6-7

You have the freedom to lay your burdens at the cross, which is wonderful. But this creates the demand that you go ever further to advance your influence upon those with whom you come into contact. While it lies solely on you to choose to be the beacon of Christian inspiration in your relationships, scripture is clear that this is how you are to act.

"In the same way, let your light shine before
others, that they may see your good
deeds and glorify your Father in
heaven."

— Matthew 5:16

And look at this verse that so clearly sums up the role of the first responder, Psalms 82: 3-4, "*Defend the weak and the fatherless; uphold the cause of the poor and the oppressed. 4. Rescue the weak and the needy; deliver them from the hand of the wicked.*" You are called to present yourself in such a manner that brings honor and glory to the Lord. The scripture does not quantify that your behavior is based on whether the person you are dealing with does or does not know if you are a Christian. This is the standard set forth for you. Trust in the Lord and let Him lift you into the place where this standard is attainable.

BE THE LIGHT

You have been personally called to be the salt and the light in this world in 1 Corinthians 4:6, *"For God, who said, 'Let light shine out of darkness,' made his light shine in our hearts to give us the light of the knowledge of the glory of God in the face of Christ."* Every Christian has been called to this, but you have the potential to be incredibly influential.

You can literally bring light into the darkness. On every single call you interact with a broken person who is either lost, struggling, or in blatant rebellion to God's law. You are called to bear the light of none other than God Himself to these people.

What does being the light in the darkness to a broken person in a fallen world look like? Colossians 3: 23-24 gives us clear instruction, *"Whatever you do, work at it with all your heart, as working for the Lord, not for human masters, 24. since you know that you will receive an inheritance from the Lord as a reward. It is the Lord Christ you are serving."*

It can be as simple as giving a panhandler a smile and a fist bump. Is there anything wrong with taking fifteen minutes to share a hamburger with the wheelchair-bound disabled veteran who always sits in front of Walmart? Is there any law preventing you from asking to pray with a pregnant homeless teenager?

As Christians, we have been instructed to treat people as the children of God, as stated in Hebrews 6:10, *"God is not unjust: he will not forget your work and the love you have shown him as you have helped his people and continue to help them."* Impressing our supervisors, coworkers, or the myriad other reasons why we do things are woefully inadequate when we consider the standard to which scripture calls us. Ephesians 6:6 says, *"Obey them not only to win their favor when their eye is on you, but as slaves of Christ, doing the will of God from your heart."*

This should be the underlying consideration when dealing with 'those' individuals. You know the individuals I'm talking about. Those people you deal with who are a drain on your patience but who have not done anything technically 'wrong.' Proverbs 15:3 says, *"The eyes of the Lord are everywhere, keeping watch on the wicked and the good."* Christ is the ultimate judge of all. This profession develops an inflated sense of importance in many.

As we read in Philippians 2:3-4, we are reminded to *"Do nothing out of selfish ambition or vain conceit. Rather, in humility value others above yourselves, 4. not looking to your own interests but each of you to the interests of the others."* If you remember that Christ *will judge you,* along with those nuisance people, you may be more aware of your flaws. (Sorry to break it to you, but... You are flawed, I am flawed, your pastor is flawed, everyone on the planet is flawed.)

Being the light does not mean you have to make grandiose statements of faith every time you encounter someone in need. While there is nothing wrong with having your bible in your work bag (it's a great way to get in some extra reading during lulls in calls for service), do you have to have it with you at work? Of course not. Neither do you have to make it a spectator sport when you pray, as we are reminded by reading Matthew 6:4, *"(b)Then your Father, who sees what is done in secret, will reward you."* Remember what Jesus said about public prayer in the parable of the Pharisee and the Tax Collector.

You bring light to your coworkers in the form of peace

amidst chaos. You bring order where there is confusion. You bring hope and joy when there is negativity. You have the light and the wisdom of God working for you. You need to recognize and accept that you are a light bearer. This is your identity and your charge.

This is the essence of your call. Accept who you are and commit to bringing the light amidst the darkest situation. This may seem daunting, but you must remember this light does not originate from within yourself. You are simply called to reflect the eternal light that has been shining since the foundation of the world, which will keep shining long after you retire. You are not the originator of the light, hope, peace, or wisdom of Christ. You are only His ambassador.

STRENGTH IN HUMILITY

Micah 6:8 says, *"He has shown you, O mortal, what is good. And what does the LORD require of you? To act justly and to love mercy and to walk humbly with your God."* Being humble in spirit in this profession can be an extremely difficult accomplishment. This profession draws Type-A personalities that are accustomed to having attention paid to them. You might fall into this category.

If you do, there is nothing wrong with that. There is a reason why this type of personality is so successful in this career field. It takes a confident person to do the things you do every day. You draw much of your confidence from your ability; luckily, you do not have to rely on your own strength to humble yourself.

One of the most effective ways to humble yourself in your relationships is through your speech. You have the freedom to speak in any manner you wish. The scripture is very clear that you have the freedom to live out every aspect of your life free from the guilt and shame set forth in the Mosaic law, but look at what the Psalmist writes in Psalm 141:3, *"Set a guard over my mouth, Lord; keep watch over the door of my lips."*

This is not to say that you are unable to use the sort of language a situation requires in dealing with certain subjects, as long as you do not blaspheme the Spirit while doing so. There are differences in the way you will have to speak to someone who is non-compliant in your efforts to place them under arrest, under the influence of any number of substances or suffering some mental or psychotic episode, and how you speak to victims, witnesses, other first responders, friends, and family. This is not a mandate but simply a suggestion for an area of your life over which you have 100% complete control.

Adhering to the Standard

This is one of the many points on which the dichotomy of our faith and our profession intersect. James 3:2 says, *"We all stumble in many ways. Anyone who is never at fault in what they say is perfect, able to keep their whole body in check."* The only one who has ever been able to perfectly do this is Christ. In Ephesians 5:4 (ESV), Paul says, *"Let there be no filthiness nor foolish talk nor crude joking, which are out of place, but instead let there be thanksgiving."*

Have you ever experienced a coworker who refuses to swear while conversing with others? It is impactful. I have a very good friend who is a California Highway Patrol Officer. We attended the same church for years, and our daughters were nationally-ranked runners who caused us to travel to races nationwide. I noticed how he spoke to people of different socio-economic strata while at cross country and track meets, in hotels, or in restaurants. He has a very quick wit yet always is respectful. When asked, he said he never uses curse words, foul language, or overtly dirty innuendo.

He refrains from these topics in every aspect of his life, not just at work. He said that non-first responder friends and coworkers have approached him to let him know how much of an inspiration he has been to them over the past decades. These folks say it is refreshing to hear someone who can joke and banter with the crew without resorting to four-letter words.

This is in line with Proverbs 15:1-2, "*A gentle answer turns away wrath, but a harsh word stirs up anger. 2. The tongue of the wise adorns knowledge, but the mouth of the fool gushes folly.*" When you temper your speech with unbelievers, you set an example that they do not understand. This plants a seed within them. Depending on your relationship, these people may approach you and comment on this difference. Hopefully, this will lead to Colossians 4:6, "*Let your conversation be always full of grace, seasoned with salt, so that you may know how to answer everyone.*" This way, you will know how to respond when an opportunity presents itself.

When you study the scripture, you will have answers readily available for anyone who questions or challenges your faith. And when they do question you on your faith, you will 'know how to answer everyone.' The biblical study techniques from the first chapter lay the foundation for you to have the knowledge needed to be an effective witness for Christ.

You will then build upon this to take that fearful yet all-important first step of sharing the gospel with your coworker. As stated in 2 Peter 1: 5-8, *"For this very reason, make every effort to add to your faith goodness; and to goodness, knowledge; 6. and to knowledge, self-control; and to self-control, perseverance; and to perseverance, godliness; 7. and to godliness, mutual affection; and to mutual affection, love. 8. For if you possess these qualities in increasing measure, they will keep you from being ineffective and unproductive in your knowledge of our Lord Jesus Christ."* The words you read today may help lead one of your coworkers to a saving grace and relationship with Jesus Christ.

It is imperative that you remember the truth of where your unsaved first responder colleagues, the suspects you arrest, and every other person you encounter throughout your day are headed.

> "I have seen a wicked and ruthless man
> flourishing like a luxuriant native tree,
> 36. but he soon passed away and was
> no more; though I looked for him, he
> could not be found. 37. Consider the
> blameless, observe the upright; a
> future awaits those who seek peace.
> 38. But all sinners will be destroyed;
> there will be no future for the wicked.
> 39. The salvation of the righteous
> comes from the Lord; he is their
> stronghold in time of trouble. 40. The
> Lord helps them and delivers them; he
> delivers them from the wicked and
> saves them, because they take refuge in
> him."

— Psalm 37:35-40

How do you think it will impact your approach to those you encounter if you remember the Psalmist's words? Especially concerning your coworkers? What about how you deal with your supervisor?

Are there great leaders in your organization who are not believers? I'm going to take a shot in the dark and unequivocally declare: Of course, there are. We see this in every single stratum of society, regardless of country, population area, or creed. Are there horrible leaders who proclaim to be Christians? Unfortunately, yes, there are. But there is a reverse side to this coin. There are phenomenal leaders in almost every agency who have the heart of a servant and are strong men and women of Christ. These are those rare people who are truly vested in the good of their agency, their superiors, and their subordinates.

Can you be an effective supervisor and an effective agent for Christ? Do you strive for this? Or would you rather separate your faith from your profession? Let's explore what the Bible says about Christians who find themselves in leadership positions.

There are so many variables that make up a great leader, and going into each of them is not the intention of this book. However, there are certain characteristics that Christian leaders should be exhibiting. Foremost, Christian leaders should be servant leaders.

> "Jesus called them together and said, 'You
> know that the rulers of the Gentiles
> lord it over them, and their high
> officials exercise authority over them.
> 26. Not so with you. Instead, whoever
> wants to become great among you must
> be your servant.'"

— MATTHEW 20:25-26

If you are not approaching your workplace with an outlook of servitude, you are simply not living up to the potential to which you have been called.

Leaders of first responders understand that their subordinates are dealing with extraordinary stress and pressure. Most of these stressors originate from the public they serve. However, great leaders recognize that their subordinates are also inundated with stressors from their departmental hierarchy. These leaders are not great just because they recognize departmental pressure. They are great leaders because they take actionable steps whenever possible to shield their subordinates from whatever they can. The Christian leader understands this is in keeping with Proverbs 27:23, which reads, *"Be sure you know the condition of your flocks, give careful attention to your herds."* It makes your job easier when you understand where your subordinates' stress is coming from and do what you can to mitigate it.

The Bible is constantly comparing a leader to a shepherd. A shepherd genuinely cares for the needs of his sheep. A great leader does not blindly dole out assignments and duties as they sit in their office. They attempt to take into account the issues their subordinates are dealing with and are proactive in their management.

I can see the eye-rolls and hear the groans. *"You have no idea what it's like supervising these people. It's like herding a bunch of cats sometimes."* You're right. I have absolutely no idea what it's like being a supervisor in your agency, department, or clinic. This book only tries to identify some common issues facing Christian first responders and presents a biblical way to address those issues.

> *"As a supervisor for a federal law enforcement agency, I have done things that I am 'not supposed' to do. Specifically in regard to boldly sharing Christ in the workspace, in my office, with countless subordinates.*
>
> *Within the federal government workforce culture, we are clearly instructed that we are not allowed to do this. But as you walk through any office you will see all types of banners, flyers, and events to celebrate aspects of our society and political agendas that we know to violate our beliefs. So, while they tell us that we cannot share the gospel of Jesus Christ, they encourage and endorse secular agendas, including things that come directly against the Christian faith.*
>
> *One day, I found myself talking to a subordinate who was an outspoken atheist who was going through a hell-on-earth situation. He shared his very personal struggles with me, and we spoke, at length, about faith. We respected each other, and he listened. I have found that people will always listen to your testimony. Share it. Be loving AND be bold. They deserve to know!*
>
> *On another occasion, a subordinate had initiated a conversation in the break room about the spiritual warfare that was incessantly tormenting her. Attacks that I knew to be of the enemy.*
>
> *In my experience, most Christians have little biblical knowledge about spiritual warfare, and broaching this topic can be quite challenging and uncomfortable. They think it's 'weird' and are avoidant about spiritual warfare discussions. But make no mistake: it is real and it is active right now. Ephesians 6:12 is very clear in this.*

I asked her (in the presence of her peers) if she wanted to hear my take on the experiences that she was seeking answers about. She said yes, so we carried the conversation into my office, where she proceeded to tell me what was haunting her, disrupting her rest and peace.

I began explaining what my personal experiences were with spiritual battles and what the Bible says about demonic attacks. This was clearly not an everyday topic discussed in most churches, much less a large field office for an agency within the Department of Homeland Security!

Overhearing some of the conversation, the SAC and the ASAC ultimately came into the office to inquire and listen to my intriguing conversation. I also called a Brother-in-Christ on the phone who knows a lot about spiritual warfare. I was able to provide her with effective advice on how to handle what was going on in a way that was biblically-sound, as opposed to how she had been handling the situation.

As a first responder supervisor, you have the capability to profess your faith in Christ at work, to subordinates and superiors alike, AS LONG AS it is done in a non-preachy way, boldly - but with love, while standing on the promises of God. What we have as Christians is unique. It's different, especially in today's culture. And it's available to everyone."

— *M.A. Philadelphia, PA*

So, this raises the question: Is being an effective agent for Christ in your leadership position something you strive for? Proverbs 24:10 says, *"If you falter in a time of trouble, how small is your strength!"* Believers and non-believers who are good leaders do not easily back down from a challenge.

Being a Christian who has ascended to leadership within the first responder community means you are uniquely qualified to stand up to challenges. James 1:12 says, *"Blessed is the one who perseveres under trial because, having stood the test, that person will receive the crown of life that the Lord has promised to those who love him."* Remember, you are fighting a good fight on more than one front.

What could justify this behavior if you are not actively seeking to be an effective Christian leader? Again, this is not a judgment or indictment. It is simply a challenging question. David writes in Psalms 39:1-3, *"I said, 'I will watch my ways and keep my tongue from sin; I will put a muzzle on my mouth while in the presence of the wicked.' 2. So I remained utterly silent, not even saying anything good. But my anguish increased; 3. my heart grew hot within me. While I meditated, the fire burned."* There are many examples of Christian first responders chafing under a self-enforced silence while working. Why would you voluntarily put that burden on yourself?

As the stories earlier in the chapter relate, you do not need to be animated in applying your beliefs. As someone in a leadership role, you are positioned to have an immeasurable impact down and up the chain of command. Remember, everything you do in the name of the Lord is beneficial, and everything you do to be obedient to Him is never wasted. In doing so, be reminded of Romans 8:28, which says, *"And we know that in all things God works for the good of those who love him, who have been called according to his purpose."* So, with this in mind, right now is the best time to take responsibility and make the conscious decision to improve your spiritual training.

Challenge Coin:

- Identify one coworker and resolve to pray for them daily for 30 days. After the 30 days, choose another and pray for them for 30 days. Do this for a calendar year and see how God blesses them and you.
- Identify two areas within your professional relationship sphere of influence and look for ways to be more of a Christ-like example.
- Partner with at least one Christian coworker and communicate with them weekly. If it is too difficult to do so in person, exchange emails, texts, or by other means, but commit to this and see how this influences your other work relationships.

CHAPTER THREE
PERSONAL RELATIONSHIPS

"People will be lovers of themselves, lovers
of money, boastful, proud, abusive,
disobedient to their parents, ungrateful,
unholy."

— 2 PETER 3:2

How many relationships do you know of that have been negatively affected as a direct result of employment as a first responder? There is an average divorce rate of 16.96% among all professions. The law enforcement community fares much better than expected, with an average of 14.47% of marriages ending in divorce (12% supervisor or detectives & 15.01% patrol/uniformed).

Firefighters come in slightly less with a 14.1% average. Registered Nurses double that of Law Enforcement with 28.95% and 24% for Physicians. Two professions landing in the top ten with the highest divorces are corrections supervisors at 46.9% and emergency services dispatchers at 46.6%.

> *"And let us consider how we may spur one*
> *another on toward love and good deeds,*
> *25. not giving up meeting together, as*
> *some are in the habit of doing, but*
> *encouraging one another—and all the*
> *more as you see the Day approaching."*

— Hebrews 10: 24-25

As these statistics suggest, your work in this exceedingly difficult career field can affect those you care about most. The stress you experience takes a toll, placing a burden on the people in your life. It is incredibly difficult sometimes to maintain a positive outlook on the difference you make within your community when you are in constant contact with the dregs of your community. When was the last time you had a positive encounter with a community member that uplifted you?

But what about the unintentional influence this job has over your personal relationships? The muck and mire in which you walk sticks to you. And no matter how hard you scrub, bits of the filth hold on to you like they have been glued. They stick to the crevices of your soul. Over time, these bits are so fully intertwined into who you are that it should come as no surprise that you have been changed. But this change does not only affect you.

The completely understandable armor you have built over the years to protect you from the daily spiritual attacks at work becomes harder and harder to take off when you cross the threshold into your home. Inevitably, this leads to a decreased empathy for the trials your spouse deals with, a decreased interest in your kids or their activities, and reduced true communication between yourself and those within your inner circle. You may find yourself increasingly fixated on the macabre while you shift your circle of friends to those who work in the same field.

CHOOSE YOUR FRIENDS WISELY

While there is nothing wrong with the inevitable shifting of your friends to those who share the same experiences as you, it is naïve to assume the people you choose to have in your life will not be a major influence on you. Proverbs 27:17 says, *"As iron sharpens iron, so one person sharpens another."* It does not say that this sharpening will be easy. Think about what happens when you sharpen something. The original material is ground down, violently stripping away those imperfections that keep it from being the best tool it could possibly be.

While this is what we are called to do in order to help our brothers and sisters in Christ become more effective, the way we accomplish this is from a position of love, like a medical provider scrubbing the dead tissue and infection from a severe wound. Knowing that God is either using you to refine someone else or He is using someone else to refine you will keep you in a biblically based mindset. This mindset allows you to accept the pain of the refinement with patience and the responsibility of refining someone else with grace and humility.

Understanding that your circle of friends will influence you should direct you towards the types of people you seek to associate with. 1 Corinthians 15:33 says, *"Do not be misled: "Bad company corrupts good character."* This is why it is so imperative to surround yourself with men and women of integrity, wisdom, and a love for the Lord.

> *"If we claim to have fellowship with him and*
> *yet walk in the darkness, we lie and do*
> *not live out the truth. 7. But if we walk*
> *in the light, as he is in the light, we have*
> *fellowship with one another, and the*
> *blood of Jesus, his Son, purifies us from*
> *all sin."*
>
> — 1 JOHN 1:6-7

Remember, your identity does not lie in your position as a first responder. You are a holy, righteous, and redeemed child of God. 1 Corinthians 1:30-31 says, *"It is because of him that you are in Christ Jesus, who has become for us wisdom from God—that is, our righteousness, holiness and redemption. 31 Therefore, as it is written: "Let the one who boasts boast in the Lord."* Your identity rests completely in the Lord.

RECONCILING RELATIONSHIPS

How do you go about repairing those close relationships you have damaged? One of the first things is recognizing that you have hurt some of the people you love. More often than not, the hurt you caused was unintentional. But this does not lessen the pain of the offended party. Next, there must be a willingness to change. You are reading this book, so... go ahead and check off that box. The third thing you should realize is that developing these habits and coping mechanisms took a long time.

It may take a long time to change them. Finally, it is important to realize that as strong as you may be, there is no way to make true repentant change without turning to

Jesus Christ. Paul talks about something much deeper than behavior modification. He writes in Ephesians 4:25-32, *"Therefore each of you must put off falsehood and speak truthfully to your neighbor, for we are all members of one body. 26. 'In your anger do not sin': Do not let the sun go down while you are still angry, 27. and do not give the devil a foothold. 28. Anyone who has been stealing must steal no longer, but must work, doing something useful with their own hands, that they may have something to share with those in need. 29. Do not let any unwholesome talk come out of your mouths, but only what is helpful for building others up according to their needs, that it may benefit those who listen. 30. And do not grieve the Holy Spirit of God, with whom you were sealed for the day of redemption. 31. Get rid of all bitterness, rage and anger, brawling and slander, along with every form of malice. 32. Be kind and compassionate to one another, forgiving each other, just as in Christ God forgave you."*

Most secular behavior modification is designed to either gain a reward for positive behavior or as an aversion of risk. Anyone can choose to stop stealing and begin giving to the poor. Think Ebenezer Scrooge. Salvation is not a requirement for someone to stop lying and begin telling the truth. Anyone can choose to stop being rude and treat people gently and with respect. More and more people are choosing to turn away from their bitterness, letting go of their rage and anger, slanderousness, brawling, and all other forms of malice. The vast majority are doing this without seeking a relationship with Jesus Christ.

"I know many close to me believe I came from a strong, Christ-centered family, but the truth is we never really knew Christ growing up. Though my mother made sure

that we heard the message every Sunday, we lived like atheists Monday through Saturday and sometimes on Sunday too. Despite the dysfunction in my family, my mother's faith in Christ alone was enough to plant a small mustard seed of faith in my heart as a young child, one that I would come back to years later. During my young adulthood, I went to war, I saw death, and I grew a hard shell. I was numb. The way that I interacted with my family was cold and distant. It was hard for me to have anything beyond a superficial relationship with anyone.

My guard was always up. As I grew older, my life became full with blessings, a loving wife who saw past my hard shell, a job in Law Enforcement, and a small home to start our life together. But I did not have peace. The fuller my life became the more crippling the fear that I would lose it all became. So, I came back to that mustard seed, and through His word, my heart began to soften. I began to pray persistently like I never had before. I became diligent in reading the Bible. I worked on developing a real personal relationship with our Father Jesus Christ. I finally felt myself building a strong enough foundation for my faith to grow. It changed my relationships with everyone. I even began to have deep conversations with my co-workers about faith, family, and friendships. A few co-workers gathering to fellowship grew into a work ministry where people in our field could share relevant life issues, prayer requests, and spiritual strength.

As I grew in my faith, my wife began to feel uneasy with the changes she saw in me. Julia came from a family that chose to live a life without God. She identified herself as agnostic and she was scared about how my expectations for her and for our marriage might shift. I did quietly pray for her, but I did not know if Julia would ever come to faith. In fact, it was many years into our marriage, just after our second child was born, that a mustard seed would be planted in her heart. There we sat at the doctor's office. He had just told us that he had found a mass in the center of my brain.

He explained that it could be a cyst, in which case I would be fine, no treatment needed, or it could be a tumor. He stopped short of explaining what a brain tumor could mean for me because, by that time, Julia, who was holding our 4-month-old son, began to cry hard, knowing exactly what the doctor intended to say. She looked at me with tear-filled eyes, and all I could feel was grateful. I was grateful that God had blessed me with such a beautiful life. When she tells the story now, she says that that was the moment she knew that I was right. Jesus' love can fill you with a peace beyond all understanding. She prayed for the first time in her life. The seed was planted.

After many years of invasive exams and MRIs, I was given good news by my doctor that I had a cyst, not a tumor, which, considering it was located in the middle of my brain, was a miracle. In addition, I had been blessed with a third, beautiful, healthy child, something I thought I may never see following what seemed like a bleak initial prognosis years before. It was in this period of more blessings that Julia confided in me that her faith was wavering. Had she only clung to Jesus when she feared for my life out of desperation? I struggled to find the right words to encourage her.

It was then that I received a last-minute email from Carlos, a good brother and a member of our work ministry. It was a reminder about the Harvest Crusade. His email could not have come at a better time. At first, it was just an excuse for my wife and I to see some of our favorite bands and escape from the world for a date night. However, I never expected that day would be the day I had been praying for so long. After almost a decade of asking the Lord to intervene, He answered my prayers. After living without faith for 32 years, Julia committed her life to Jesus, and not just privately, but publicly, in front of thousands of people during the Harvest Crusade at Angels Stadium, and later, to her family.

It is humbling that Jesus used the mustard seed of faith that grew in me to help create a work ministry that now provides fellowship for other believers in Law Enforcement and their families. Christ gave me the courage to walk openly in my faith in my personal and professional life which ultimately led to my wife's walk with Christ today."

— *D.J.~ Lake Forest, CA*

This officer was able to overcome some pretty extreme emotional and spiritual obstacles. His submission to Christ and willingness to trust in His plan were instrumental in leading his wife to the saving grace of God's love.

Lay It All Down

Congratulations on humbling yourself and admitting that you have to change at a fundamental level. This ability to look within oneself and recognize that a change is needed is probably one of the hardest steps to take for a hard-charging first responder such as yourself. This journey will become easier with each corresponding step you take on this restorative path. Before you know it, you will find yourself running toward the one who provides perfect comfort.

> "Anyone who falls on this stone will be
>   broken to pieces; anyone on whom it
>   falls will be crushed."
>
> — MATTHEW 21:44

You are taking the step to be one who falls on the rock, and you will be so very much the better for it.

How many years did it take for this hard shell to develop around your soul? Two years? Five? If it took any longer than five years for this hardness to set in then you, my friend, are the exception to the rule. Again, this is why the average law enforcement career only lasts seven years. Fitness and nutrition experts state that healthy weight loss should be done at a rate between 0.5 and two pounds per week. Anything less than half a pound will not have any consequential benefit. More than two pounds of weight loss per week can lead to other health issues and may not result in long-term fitness.

This means it would take you anywhere from six months to two years to lose fifty extra pounds. My first medical assignment after Hospital Corpsman school was the pediatric clinic at the Naval Hospital San Diego. This was the early 90s, and I can recall the Doctors advising new mothers that it would take two months to recover for every month of pregnancy. You may ask how this physiologic metric correlates to our spiritual fitness. God has the authority and the ability to miraculously and immediately transform one's soul. Still, for most people, this process may take years before taking root deep enough for your loved ones to see effectual change.

Changing one's perspective is the beginning of changing one's outlook. Colossians 3:12-14 says,

"Therefore, as God's chosen people, holy and dearly loved, clothe yourselves with compassion, kindness, humility, gentleness and patience. 13. Bear with each other and forgive one another if any of you has a grievance against someone. Forgive as the Lord forgave you. 14. And over all these virtues put on love, which binds them all together in perfect unity." The Lord has called us to view people differently than the world views them. Just imagine the impact you would have on your family and friends if you started forgiving like this!

As a Christian first responder, you are probably familiar with John 15:13, *"Greater love has no one than this: to lay down one's life for one's friends."* But, look at what Jesus says in John 15:12, 14: *"My command is this: Love each other as I have loved you... 14. You are my friends if you do what I command."* Jesus has commanded us to live a better life than those in the world by loving people in a way that transcends the way the world loves. One of the ways to accomplish this is to live out Ephesians 4:2, *"Be completely humble and gentle; be patient, bearing with one another in love."*

While this is generally applied to your relationships with other believers, living like this towards non-believers is the embodiment of other parts of the gospel.

> "But do this with gentleness and respect,
> 16. keeping a clear conscience, so that
> those who speak maliciously against
> your good behavior in Christ may be
> ashamed of their slander."
>
> — 1 Peter 3:15b-16

Approaching people with an attitude of love embodies

and affirms their lives and shows the individual person has meaning and value. The value of love is taking on the ownership of improving your life and the life of someone else.

SPEAKING TRUTH WITH GRACE

Speaking truth to people can be a brutal event and one that can be bitter for everyone involved. This is especially true the more intimate the relationship is between the truth-speaker and the one(s) being spoken to. Speaking the truth is intended to scour out resentment between those involved, like a healthcare worker debriding the dead flesh out of a severe wound. This pain is sometimes necessary to heal, but it is unpleasant. Biblical truth, spoken through an attitude of love, is the best structure to build a lasting relationship.

Thank God in heaven above that you do not have to rely on your own strength and ability to obey this command!

> "So Christ himself gave the apostles, the prophets, the evangelists, the pastors and teachers, 12. to equip his people for works of service, so that the body of Christ may be built up 13. until we all reach unity in the faith and in the knowledge of the Son of God and become mature, attaining to the whole measure of the fullness of Christ."

> — EPHESIANS 4:11-13

Getting plugged into a local church and small group study are the biblically prescribed answers to guard against the hardening of your heart. Proverbs 17:17 says, *"A friend loves at all times, and a brother is born for a time of adversity."* Plug yourself into your local church and find mentors who can help you navigate the pitfalls that will spring up along your journey.

The Joy of the Lord Is Our Strength

Your relationship with God should be the ultimate source of all your joy.

> "The kingdom of heaven is like treasure
>   hidden in a field. When a man found it,
>   he hid it again, and then in his joy went
>   and sold all he had and bought that
>   field."
>
> — Mathew 13:44

The truth of this is not diminished in any way if you are married. God is still the ultimate source of your joy. However, if you are married, you should count your blessings daily. Proverbs 18:22 says, *"He who finds a wife finds what is good and receives favor from the Lord."* This means that your spouse is your most intimate worldly relationship, so the bond you share must be protected at all costs. This is firmly established as we read Genesis 2:24, *"That is why a man leaves his father and mother and is united to his wife, and they become one flesh."*

Being honest with your spouse necessitates informing them when stressors are coming home from work.

> "A wife of noble character who can find?
> She is worth far more than rubies. 11.
> Her husband has full confidence in her
> and lacks nothing of value."
>
> — PROVERBS 31:10-11

If King Solomon is to be believed, you must have 'full confidence' in your spouse. Does it show you believe the words of the wisest man to have ever lived when you shut down communication from your spouse, even if it was with the best intentions? You are not protecting your spouse from the troubling things you witness at your job by refusing to talk about them. As noble as your intentions may have been when you shut out your most intimate partner from such an impactful part of your life, you inadvertently tell them they are incapable of helping you.

At the beginning of your career, this may not have been how either of you viewed this informational shutting out. Heck, both of you may have even been grateful: you for the solace and comfort of talking about everyday things, they for the blissful ignorance of the true dangers of your job. While you may not notice it at first, a wedge develops in the relationship that slowly starts to splinter the very thing you were trying to protect. You will begin to keep up those work barriers around the house, especially when the discussion is about work topics. Your spouse will become resentful, which may morph into a full-blown bitterness about the lack of communication and reluctance to discuss work issues.

By the time you are a decade into this career, you might find yourself divorced, in counseling, or living a joyless existence at home and work. How many coworkers do you know who have been involved with extramarital affairs, developed unhealthy addictions, or become workaholics? I bet if you dug far enough into the issue, you would find the primary root cause of their marital collapse was a lack of intimate communication. I would even go so far as to say that this lack of communication started at, or near, the beginning of their first responder career. No one who identifies as a Christian first responder ever intentionally starts their day wanting to cheat on their spouse, develop a drug or alcohol addiction, or find themselves morally bankrupt. This is the manifestation of the proverbial 'slippery slope.'

Love Your Spouse and Children Well

You know your spouse better than anyone else in the world. And they know you better than any other person in the world. Ecclesiastes 4:9-11 is a good reminder: *"Two are better than one, because they have a good return for their labor: 10. If either of them falls down, one can help the other up. But pity anyone who falls and has no one to help them up. 11. Also, if two lie down together, they will keep warm. But how can one keep warm alone?"*

This does not mean that you have to tell your spouse every gory detail about each accident, shooting, violent assault, or senseless act you see humans do to each other on a daily basis. You are smart enough to gauge how much to divulge regarding your work experiences. But share you must. It is imperative to maintaining a healthy level of intimacy in your relationship. Giving your spouse access to such a vulnerable part of yourself lets them know how much you trust them.

This trust conveys a new level of respect for your

spouse's capabilities. When you begin to discuss topics that had previously been taboo, you are relaying three important and distinct ideas to your spouse. First, they are strong enough to handle the topic. Regardless of what event you are discussing, simply talking about it with your spouse lets them know you regard them as emotionally capable of walking this path with you.

Secondly, you convey to your spouse that they are smart enough to have an insightful opinion. When you discuss the event with them, you are saying that their interpretation of the situation has meaning, and you value their perception and intuition. Thirdly, and maybe most important to the relationship, you let them know they are important to you. By sharing these experiences with your spouse, you directly validate their worth to you as a partner and confidant.

When you attempt to protect your spouse, you are saying the exact opposite. You are telling them they are not very mentally capable, they are not emotionally strong, and they are not really that valuable to you—

> "You have stolen my heart, my sister, my
> bride; you have stolen my heart with
> one glance of your eyes, with one jewel
> of your necklace. 10. How delightful is
> your love, my sister, my bride! How
> much more pleasing is your love than
> wine, and the fragrance of your
> perfume more than any spice!"

> — SONG OF SOLOMON 4:9-10

We must once again start treating our spouses as if they

have stolen our hearts with but a glance and finding them more intoxicating than the finest wine.

In the same way, your children are a gift from God and should be included in your innermost confidence. We are encouraged to remember this when reading Psalm 127:3-4, "*Children are a heritage from the Lord, offspring a reward from him. 4. Like arrows in the hands of a warrior are children born in one's youth.*" No matter how many children you have, realize that they are individually made by the God of the universe specifically for you. And yes, this applies to your adopted children, step-children, and special needs children. Psalm 139:13-14 says, "*For you created my inmost being; you knit me together in my mother's womb. 14. I praise you because I am fearfully and wonderfully made; your works are wonderful, I know that full well.*" Again, this point is reiterated in James 1:17, "*Every good and perfect gift is from above, coming down from the Father of the heavenly lights, who does not change like shifting shadows.*" If you have children, you have been given one of the most sacred earthly responsibilities. You are responsible for shaping a human life.

This is not a book about how to raise your child. There are tens of thousands of those, written by much more qualified people than I. Raising a child is an awesome responsibility, and it is just another aspect exacerbated by your being a first responder. There are so many passages in the Bible dealing with how to raise children. As first responders, we have an extremely different outlook on how to raise kids. This can result in vastly different ways in which you approach your responsibility.

Keeping between these two guideposts from Proverbs and Ephesians can only help. On the port side, you have Proverbs 22:6, "*Start children off on the way they should go, and even when they are old they will not turn from it."* The starboard boundary can be found in Ephesians 6:4, *"Fathers, do not exasperate your children; instead, bring them up in the training and instruction of the Lord."* Train them in the fear of the Lord, and create an environment where they have the freedom to grow within the rules you set forth. Seems simple enough, right? Well, by now, you should know how hard it is to complete the simple things for which the Bible has called you. Luckily, there is somewhere for you to go, as found in Psalm 121:1-2, *"I lift up my eyes to the mountains—where does my help come from? 2. My help comes from the Lord, the Maker of heaven and earth."* Does it get any better than that?

COMPLETE DEPENDENCY ON CHRIST

Reliance on the Lord is a difficult thing to wrap the mind around for many first responders. You are accustomed to being the emotional fortress during times of crises and chaos. While the truth of this statement does not change, you know that you must have a place to go where you can be refreshed. Many first responders seek this release in the bottle, in other people, or in pursuing some activity or hobby. While there is nothing wrong with each of these things, they will never provide the satisfaction, stability, or relief found in Christ Jesus. Look at what the bible says about Jesus as the source of comfort. Psalms 46:1 says, *"God is our refuge and strength, an ever-present help in trouble."* The truth of this passage makes alcohol, affirmation, and activity pale by comparison.

While there is nothing wrong with imbibing alcohol, when a first responder first pursues comfort in the bottle, there is an initial release. This feeling of relief is magnified when drinking with coworkers or other first responders. How many of your colleagues would like to go to a 'cop bar' or 'unit bar' together when the shift ends? The deputies from the local department I served with would call this 'choir practice.'

The camaraderie that can develop during these outings is an amazing morale boost. It begins to feel like these are the only people who could ever possibly know what it's like to walk the line you walk. This is one of the reasons military teams and firefighters are such tight-knit units. Ultimately, what started as something you participated in once every six weeks or so begins to happen every few weeks. Then, every other week. Then, every week, until you are going out almost every day before going home. As the quick trips to the bar increase in frequency, so too does the amount of alcohol needed in order to 'take the edge off.' You know where this road eventually leads.

Again, there is nothing wrong in and of itself with dating or seeking friendships outside of the family for those first responders who are married. Unfortunately, too many first responders end up as serial daters or begin relationships that interfere with their spousal and familial relationships.

How many coworkers do you know that just can't seem to 'find the one' or are constantly 'out with the boys'? Again, there is nothing wrong with either of these in and of themselves. Remember what the Bible says in Proverbs 13:20, *"Walk with the wise and become wise, for a companion of fools suffers harm."* This is where pursuing friendships within your local church can significantly bless your life. These friends can tell you when you are starting to veer off course.

Hobbies and the like have been given to us by the Lord for you to participate and enjoy. You are free to pursue whatever is your passion. And that freedom allows you to pursue your hobby with gusto. But like all gifts from the Lord, these enjoyments are not intended to replace our pursuit of the Lord. Too often, the gift overshadows the giver when it comes to pursuing hobbies. There is a fine line between pursuing a passion and developing an obsession.

You are responsible for knowing where that line lies in your own life. One of the easiest ways to determine if your hobby has superseded your relationship with Jesus is if you put off reading the Bible in order to do just one more mile, stock trade, repetition, video game level, song, tune-up, or whatever aspect your hobby entails. Again, let me stress: there is nothing wrong with pursuing these passions in and of themselves. So go out there and crush that Caber Toss PR! But don't forget to read your bible, pray, and thank God that He put this passion in your life.

One of the juxtapositions of our profession is the reversal of the fabric of life. What I mean by this is that our ideal world, the very things for which we strive and sacrifice, ultimately, is the comfort and balance of a good life. Picture your most idyllic times. Imagine, if you will, sitting in your favorite recliner in front of the fireplace, and the kids are reading in a corner or playing on the floor. You are all enjoying a giant mug of steaming hot chocolate while snow falls on the other side of the big bay windows. I know this is not every person's ideal world. The 'good life' looks different to each of us.

But when we don that uniform each day (and yes, plain clothes are a uniform) and go out into the chaotic uncertainty of a new shift, we voluntarily exchange our ideal world for an ever-changing unknown. I mean, let's face it: this is exactly what many first responders profess as the reason why they love their job. And why it is so hard to retire once that becomes an option. We are excited by the myriad of things that can happen at any given time while on the job. Here is where the juxtaposition comes into play.

After a while, we become more comfortable in the chaos. We become more anxious, irritable, and emotionally and physically detached from the very people, events, and way of life we are desperately trying to protect. When this happens, we seek increasingly risky ways to spend our time in our ideal world. I have personally pursued or know first responders who have engaged in full-contact stick fighting, motorcycle racing, parachuting, white water kayaking, mountaineering/rock climbing, and free diving. The key here is to recognize that this profession is a calling, and in answering that call, we choose to live a portion of our lives on the fringe of acceptable society. We voluntarily step into the chaos to preserve order. It is truly a rare soul who can walk this fine line, day in and day out, without the darkness infecting the light.

The great news is Christ has shown us a way to do it. Not only that, He provided His Spirit to help us overcome the dimming of the light. Recognizing that this is occurring and having the humility to take appropriate action steps to undo this switch in our home life are two of the hardest realities of the Christian first responder. We are 'Alphas,' and we are used to fixing the problem. So, this begs the question: Does it really make us any less effective, or is there anything wrong with seeking the resources to fix a problem within our own lives?

How can shifting your outlook back towards a Christ-centric focus just a little bit affect positive results in your personal relationships? 1 Corinthians 15:58 says, *"Therefore, my dear brothers and sisters, stand firm. Let nothing move you. Always give yourselves fully to the work of the Lord, because you know that your labor in the Lord is not in vain."* The moment you adjust how you perceive the reward for your work so that you truly want whatever glory you may earn to go to Christ is precisely the time you will see big results in other parts of your life. The relationships with your spouse, children, siblings, friends, and church family will all blossom as a result of this intentional shift of focus.

How does one break these habits and start to change their focus? This is one of the many beauties of Christianity. While we do have to put in work, our hope does not rely on our own effort. All we have to do is bring our request to the God of the Universe. Philippians 4:19 reminds us, *"And my God will meet all your needs according to the riches of his glory in Christ Jesus."* Everything we need to effect positive change in our personal relationships lies in the very person in whom we find our salvation. How incredibly awesome is that?

While individual results may vary, this is one of the only actions that guarantee a return on your investment. You will receive blessing upon blessing when you live a life focused more intently on Jesus Christ. And while some people will be able to dive in and make a 180-degree change of course, there is nothing wrong with making incremental adjustments over time.

Just like the recommendation made concerning your physical and spiritual conditioning, the goal is progress, not perfection. As the Chinese philosopher Laozi's famous proverb says, *"A journey of a thousand miles begins with a single step."* Start with a single change. Identify milestones along the way. You will become stronger the farther you go. When the journey finally ends, you will look back in amazement at how far you have gone. Oh, and by the way.

The journey only ends when you are with Christ in paradise.

The promise we strive for is found in Isaiah 25:8 but also echoed in Revelation 21: 4, *"He will wipe every tear from their eyes. There will be no more death"* or mourning or crying or pain, for the old order of things has passed away."* After a lifetime of fighting in the trenches, when you go to heaven, you will forever be free from the pain, misery, and fear that was such a marked part of your daily life. You will never again be battered, bruised, reviled, or disdained simply because of your work in a certain type of profession. Our promise as peacemakers is that our heavenly reward will be enormous, and this promise is found in Matthew 5:9, *"Blessed are the peacemakers, for they will be called children of God."*

Challenge Coin:

- What are some of the things keeping you from opening up to your spouse about what you experience on the job? How can you and your spouse be more open to discussing what goes on at work?
- Identify three non-work-related things that take you away from time with your family. In what way can you shift your priority towards increasing quality time with your family?
- Identify three areas of your life that will improve by giving glory to Christ. How can you go about making incremental steps to increase focusing on Christ?

Chapter Four
Death: The End Result Of Violence

"Save me, O God, for the waters have come
up to my neck. I sink in the miry
depths, where there is no foothold. I
have come into the deep waters; the
floods engulf me. I am worn out calling
for help; my throat is parched. My eyes
fail, looking for my God."

— Psalm 69: 1-3

There is not a single aspect of the first responder community in which death and loss do not touch. The evil that is expressed through violence and the senselessness of traumatic events is the biggest contributing factor to first responder fatigue. This disillusionment is akin to the individual first responder being infected with a virus. This burnout leads to a whole host of other issues. These issues are found within the first responder community and have a ripple effect in areas outside the first responder's department or agency. This, in turn, affects the first responders' immediate and extended family, church group, and circle of friends.

There is a reason why the average length of a law enforcement career is only seven years. Firefighters fare a bit better, primarily due to their ability to work through the traumatic event with their peers (who were exposed to the same stressors) at the firehouse. I come from a predominantly law enforcement family; however, one of my nephews spent several years as a fire cadet. While the fire department did a very good job limiting the cadet's exposure to some of the more grotesque and severe incidents, they did not shy away from showing them the realities of being a firefighter.

It was enough for my nephew to choose a different career path. This is not a criticism of my nephew. He was a big, strong, tough young man who played every single down (offense and defense) of every football game of his senior year. He has since grown into a big, strong, tough man who loves his family and provides a great life for them. His decision not to go into the fire academy was one born of a maturity rarely seen in one's youth.

Death, Trauma, and Violence

Dealing with trauma and violence is one of the most difficult aspects of working as a first responder. This is true regardless of the capacity, geographic location, or socioeconomic makeup of your assigned area. Yes, I am claiming that a death in Helena, Montana, affects a first responder the same as a death in Baltimore, Maryland. I spoke with a dispatcher from Omaha, Nebraska, who was happy to talk but did not want to be quoted. What he said clearly illustrates this point. He spoke about working from rural areas to big cities and everything in between.

He explained how first responders in smaller communities have a much more difficult time than their larger agency counterparts might realize. These smaller agencies deal with all of the trauma, fighting, death, drugs, and gang issues that any big city agency does. The only differences are in the frequency of incidents and the lack of availability of assistance. While the smaller communities may not see these big issues on a daily basis, they are generally the only officers dealing with them. These officers have very little backup assistance on calls when things 'go south.'

Each category of first responder experiences people who have been the victim of assaults, traumatic accidents, shootings, suicides, sexual assaults, child abuse and exploitation, human trafficking, spousal abuse, homicide, and elder abuse. The list of tragic incidents to which first responders are exposed has the literal potential to go on and on, ad nauseam.

Law Enforcement Officers are on the front lines of many of these events, wading into the fray while the perpetrators of such violence are still active. Firefighters experience death on a large scale, often witnessing the death or physical destruction of whole families. Emergency Medical personnel work frantically to save the lives of the victims of these violent events. Hospital-based medical personnel continue the life-saving care and must then follow that care into recovery.

"In 2008, I was working as a Deputy at Jefferson County Sheriff's Department, Colorado in Detentions. I was assigned to medium and maximum security most of

the time but on this particular Tuesday night I was working in the work release unit, a minimum-security classification. In work release, the inmates have jobs outside of the jail and pay 10% of their income to the program for rent. At about 0200 hours, I heard a radio call from my fellow Deputy next door to me that he had an inmate on a bunk who was unresponsive and not breathing.

A deputy from another module and I ran over, grabbed the mattress, and carefully but quickly set him on the floor. We grabbed an AED and began CPR. As we were alternating chest compressions, administering breaths and following AED prompts I could see the inmate dying right in front of me. We continued until the Fire Department arrived and we released him into their care.

Later on, my shift Sergeant told me that the inmate was deceased upon arrival at the local hospital. The inmate was morbidly obese, had heart issues, and had too many energy drinks in his system which brought on a heart attack. I remember thinking about how quickly that inmate transitioned out of this life. One minute he was alive on his bunk and the next he was gone.

My faith was then as it is now completely in Jesus. In the Gospel of John, Jesus says, 'Because I live, you also shall live'. In that passage, he is referring to eternal life being found only in him. So, in my observation of the above-mentioned event that inmate passed beyond this physical world. What I don't know is did he know Jesus?

Nothing wakes up a person more than seeing someone die in front of you. Ever since that event, I try to keep the perspective that God is the only answer in the midst of a troubled world, and it doesn't matter how polished or tarnished our lives are. It only matters that we walk with The Savior of The World, because when our time on Earth is done the only one that can save us from our sins and usher us into true eternal life is Jesus."

— *Z.G. DENVER, CO*

Unfortunately, this societal tendency towards violence is nothing new. The first overt crime against another person was not a theft or sexual assault. The third person to ever walk the earth became jealous of and murdered the fourth-ever person on earth. This act was not an accident or crime of passion immediate to the perceived insult. When Cain killed Abel, it was a premeditated, well thought out crime committed with the express purpose of benefiting the perpetrator and depriving the victim.

Have you ever noticed how Cain immediately went from having his sacrifice rejected to plotting Abel's murder? Even when God personally warned him to control his anger, Cain still thought it would be better for him to get rid of his younger brother. Cain believed that God would be pleased with his next sacrifice if Abel were not there to offer one. This is what Jesus was talking about in Mark 7:21-23, "*'21. For it is from within, out of a person's heart, that evil thoughts come—sexual immorality, theft, murder, 22. adultery, greed, malice, deceit, lewdness, envy, slander, arrogance and folly. 23. All these evils come from inside and defile a person.'*" Nearly 3,000 years later (give or take a few decades), the violence had only intensified and amplified. Look at what was written by the prophet Hosea 4:2, "*There is only cursing, lying and murder, stealing and adultery; they break all bounds, and bloodshed follows bloodshed.*" You see this played out every single day. Petty jealousies, lusts, perversions, and excess ultimately lead to the destruction of a human being.

The Depravity of Humanity

Everyone should be made aware of the depths of evil to which we all have the capacity to delve. Even Christians have the capacity to engage in the most heinous acts of cruelty and barbarism. An oft-cited example is David's illicit affair with Bathsheba and the ultimate murder of Uriah, who just so happened to be one of David's closest friends. A lesser-known example comes from the first half of World War II. In 1942, members of the German Order Police, Reserve Police Battalion 101, participated in several separate mass executions, resulting in the near extermination of Jews from several cities in Poland.

This was *after* they were given the option *NOT* to take part. Afterwards, they conducted round-ups and forced deportations to death and concentration camps. These Police Officers were, by and large, not members of the Nazi party and in their mid-30s (so they could not use the excuse of being indoctrinated into Naziism as Hitler Youth). Neither were they employed on active military service. Almost all identified as belonging to the Christian faith.

One of the reasons that many first responders have such a hard time dealing with the violence and trauma of this profession is how our society views the use of violence. Generations have spent an inordinate amount of energy ensuring the next generation understands the consequences of using violence. This has been a particular mainstay of the Western world's child-rearing lifestyle. This was such an integral part of societal norms that a group in mid-19th century England went so far as to successfully *change* the fifth commandment to '*Thou shall not kill.*'

This commandment was originally issued by God in Exodus 20:13, "*You shall not murder.*" The idiosyncrasy here seems small, but the contextual implication is huge. The act of killing someone is not the sin. The act of murdering someone is. The moral distinction here is the same with any of the other commandments: if your heart is inclined toward God and His word, then your actions will be in keeping with His will. King Solomon writes in Proverbs 4:23, *"Above all else, guard your heart, for everything you do flows from it."* This is an extremely complex theological topic, and many theologians have tackled this issue in their own books in a way much more comprehensible than I could ever have achieved.

This does not mean you have a carte blanche excuse to act however you wish, like Stalin or Henry VIII. On the contrary, this should be a sobering assessment of your motivations, thought processes, and rationales.

> *"The Lord examines the righteous, but the*
> *wicked, those who love violence, he hates*
> *with a passion."*
>
> — PSALM 11:5

Does this mean God hates you if you enjoy martial arts or get together with friends to watch fight night? Of course not. Here, the Psalmist is talking about those predators who enjoy inflicting physical and psychological pain for no other reason than their own gratification. All of you law enforcement and corrections officers know the type. You deal with them daily. The type of person who loves violence for violence's sake is as different from you (who just loves a good MMA fight) as a chimpanzee is from a silverback gorilla. Same species, different animal.

It is okay for you to start shifting your comfort of

violence back to what David says in Psalm 144:1, "*Praise be to the Lord my Rock, who trains my hands for war, my fingers for battle.*" I would go so far as to say that our society needs us to steer back to this worldview. I say this because we, as a God-fearing society, need to raise men who are capable of violence but understand when to employ it and when to restrain it.

A good man is not a gentleman.

A gentleman is weak and more inclined to harm people as a way to lash out. A truly good man is a violent man who has that violence under voluntary restraint. Understanding the truth of this statement will also allow you to be free from the self-imposed guilt that is often felt by good people who have had to use violence justifiably.

Violence is As Old As Humanity

The Bible is full of examples of humans killing other humans, and it is credited to them as righteousness. Abram rescued Lot and offered a tenth of the bounty to Melchizedek. Sampson killed 1,000 Philistines with the jawbone of a donkey. Phineas skewered the Israelite Zimri and the Midianite woman Kozbi as the plague raged in the Israeli camp. And let us not forget about the songs that were sung in the streets of Jerusalem celebrating David killing tens of thousands of Israel's enemies.

These are all well-known examples of God-fearing people taking the lives of others and it being assessed as a good thing. While it is understandable if you find it difficult to compare yourself to Samson, Abraham, or King David, could you see yourself as a Gideon, Deborah, or Shamgar (whose exploits are summed up in one verse: Judges 3:31)?

What about some of the lesser-known stories of

righteous men and women employing violence? Can you possibly identify with the story in 1 Samuel 14 on a more intimate level? 1 Samuel 14:13-14 says, "*Jonathan climbed up, using his hands and feet, with his armor-bearer right behind him. The Philistines fell before Jonathan, and his armor-bearer followed and killed behind him. 14. In that first attack Jonathan and his armor-bearer killed some twenty men in an area of about half an acre.*" Two dudes fighting in an area the size of a large suburban backyard probably seems much more relatable to you, right?

Many of you started your first responder career with service in the military. You may still be on active duty or involved with the Reserves/National Guard. In those early years, I'm probably not too far off in assuming that it was a shock to your worldview to witness the things done to other human beings by people who truly believed themselves to be of a good and decent character. Your upbringing has led you to believe that people were essentially good and 'bad people' were an anomaly.

It is a common belief in many Western Civilizations that these people were created by an act of victimization or some other traumatic personal experience that caused them to act outside the bounds of normal society. What about the first time you deployed to that third-world environment? It was there when you probably realized for the first time that the sentiments and morals you and your friends were raised with were not necessarily the case for people raised throughout most of the world. Do not get me wrong. There are wonderful people from every people group, societal norm, and country the world over. But those of you who have been 'down range' know what I am talking about.

Many of you felt fear for the first time during this first

combat deployment. I am not talking about a fear of being hurt or the fear you feel while watching a scary movie. I am talking about a visceral, gut-wrenching dread that saps the marrow from your bones and glues your tongue to the roof of your mouth. Take a look at this story from a service member who was at the Pentagon on September 11, 2001.

"When John asked me to provide a story for his book, I thought it was time I finally talked about what happened on 9/11. I have never spoken of this before and am nervous even now to relay some of the events that happened. But people need to know that faith can see you through even the most horrific days.

Fort Myer Airfield, Arlington, VA, September 11, 2001. My unit was getting ready at 0400 hours to deploy to New York City to assist with the safety and security of planned demonstrations and protests. We had drawn our weapons from the armory, donned our riot gear, and staged to depart when we heard that events had escalated. We had already witnessed the planes hitting the Twin Towers. We were ordered to stand down from the 'less-lethal' posture and assume Threat Condition Delta. While we were getting assignments to set up perimeters around the Joint Chiefs of Staff homes was when we saw a shadow over the east. This shadow goes directly into the Pentagon on the helipad side by section 66 of Arlington National Cemetery. After we had seen the Twin Towers struck in New York most of us figured our deployment there would transition into a rescue and recovery operation. None of us ever expected for the rescue and recovery to be in our backyard. As soon as the plane hit the Pentagon, several of us just ran in. As a staff NCO, I directed my troops too, and I immediately began to pull out as many people and body parts as quickly as possible. Initially, there was not any concern or consideration for the hazards. Nobody cared about toxins, carcinogens, or biohazard; nor race, creed, or religion. We all just had one task: to rescue as many people as we could. That day was the epitome of what it means to help one another.

Just about after a day, it slowly began to change to a more organized rescue effort. With the arrival of more personnel came mass casualty stations, along with the color-coded rescue and triage teams. Help came in from all around the world. Cadaver dogs, rescue dogs, firefighter task forces, special paramedics, and specialized HAZMAT and military teams had arrived and were put to work. One of the eeriest things I have ever seen was walking into a hallway, now reduced to a black tunnel, and seeing white shadows on the wall. Just a day before, these white shadows had been people going about their normal day-to-day activities. I saw starched uniforms still sitting at desks, untouched by fire or overpressure, with nobody in them. There were bodies, though, and for many of the remains, there was just the torso. The extremities were simply gone. I remember finding my friend and neighbor, Craig, still sitting at his desk. He had been badly charred, but he almost looked as if he was smiling. As a new Christian, this struck me as God's grace being passed to him in the form that he did not suffer. As I was still in my friend's office a US Marine came through yelling for everyone to leave. There was a loud growl like a lion's roar. I had to leave Craig where he was, and to this day I have regretted not being able to retrieve him. We were walking down this dark corridor towards the light. The noise was chaotic. The roar from the building, the fire engines and police cars outside with their sirens blaring, everyone yelling at everybody else to run towards the light outside. I didn't know what had happened, but I knew I had to get out of the Pentagon. Suddenly, this loud shriek like a cry overwhelmed all the other noise. A giant thing that looked almost like a hand, made of flames and smoke was hovering just under the ceiling. It shrieked as it came out of the building. I remember the look of disappointment on all of the rescuer's faces. They knew what had just happened. They started putting on different suits: white biohazard suits with full face masks and shields, helmets, and tanks. They kept saying, 'that's probably the last of the oxygen'. It was a very, very sad moment, but it was a poignant one as well. I have never before experienced the level of unity and faith that existed that day."

— *M.G., ARLINGTON, VA*

This is where many of you experienced the pain of loss and were introduced to the specter that is death. Before your first taste of combat, you probably belonged to one of two camps. You either whole-heartedly believed everything would be alright, even if you screwed up pretty badly, or you felt as though you would instantly be killed. Either way, you were confident that you would either come through the pending combat unscathed or you wouldn't have to worry about it anymore.

It was not until after you experienced combat that you realized the demoralizing truth: You or someone you care about could still die, regardless of whether you did everything right or not. And the worst realization of all: There is nothing you can do to change the outcome. This is an impotence that cuts into one's very soul and a pang of guilt that is all too often perceived as a specter that knows no relief. This is despair.

Murder vs Killing

God knew that in this fallen world, there may be a legitimate reason to take a human life. That is why His command was not to murder, as opposed to commanding us not to kill. This is an especially important point for law enforcement and military members to understand.

I recognize how this next statement may come across for many reading this book, but you must know that it is not a source of shame if you have ever been required to take another person's life. While I recognize that my combat experiences are different from those of other veterans, it was years after being in Somalia before I was able to process the truth of this statement. I had read the words but did not accept what they said. I could not fully grasp that what had happened was orchestrated by God.

While the problems associated with this thinking are multifold, one of the most blaring aspects is it limits your effectiveness to be used by God. Can you imagine how valuable you could be in the next crisis if you could accept what the Bible says without the guilt of having to do your job? Romans 13:4 says, *"For the one in authority is God's servant for your good. But if you do wrong, be afraid, for rulers do not bear the sword for no reason. They are God's servants, agents of wrath to bring punishment on the wrongdoer."* You have been ordained by the creator of the universe to perform those less-than-pleasant tasks that are required in your profession. This understanding should provide tremendous liberation from guilt for doing your job.

I also know that the guilt will be there anyway. Many of you are familiar with that little voice in your ear. You know, the one telling you, '*God can't really love you; you're a murderer.*' The same voice that says, '*You had other options. You didn't really need to kill that guy*'. You must stop listening to that voice. As hard as it may be to shut out that voice, you must. It is the voice of the accuser and those sent by him. That voice is a lie. Jesus had some harsh words about those who were used by the devil to distract those trying to follow God's plan, as we read in John 8:44, which says, "*You belong to your father, the devil, and you want to carry out your father's desires. He was a murderer from the beginning, not holding to the truth, for there is no truth in him. When he lies, he speaks his native language, for he is a liar and the father of lies.*"

I know it's easier said than done. I'm not that naive. But don't take my word for it. God the Father told the prophet in Isaiah 43:25, "*I, even I, am he who blots out your transgressions, for my own sake, and remembers your sins no more.*" When you choose to continue to put on this yoke from which you have been freed, it is self-condemnation, as read in 2 Corinthians 3:17, "*Now the Lord is the Spirit, and where the Spirit of the Lord is, there is freedom.*" You are free from the weight of guilt, not because of anything you have done, but because of and for the glory of God.

In World War I, many soldiers, sailors, and Marines experienced a condition known as Shell Shock after extended combat. While the signs, symptoms, and effects did not change in any measurable way, this condition was redesignated as Battle Fatigue for World War II and Korean War veterans. Nowadays, just about anyone who hasn't lived in a cave for the last fifty years is familiar with the term post-traumatic stress disorder (PTSD). While the names have evolved, the conditions are the same. PTSD is an injury affecting one's psyche that literally changes the way the brain processes stress. While veterans from the World Wars, Korea, and Vietnam were considered weak for developing this condition, there is a heroic movement trying to change the stigmas associated with PTSD. One of the major changes is easy enough.

Drop the D, and this is no longer a 'disorder.' Now, it is simply Post Traumatic Stress. Every single first responder has experienced stress following a traumatic event. There is also a new subject within the broader diagnosis of PTS known as Moral Injury. Recent research suggests that moral injury is a greater contributing factor to PTS than the actual event you experienced. Thus, having been raised in a first-world environment increases your propensity for suffering moral injury and PTS. If there is such a thing as a disadvantage to being born in such an amazing society, this is probably it. This does not constitute an advocacy for stopping, declining, or in any other way failing to seek any mental health treatment you need. First responders, military, and veteran populations have an epidemic suicide level, so please seek treatment.

You may not have been required to take a human life, but instead, you had a life taken from you. Everyone experiences this kind of loss. The death of a loved one can take your breath away and hurt to your marrow. It can leave you hunched over and unable to take the next step. Unfortunately, I know the pain of this all too well. Our oldest daughter has had four children, all of whom were preemies. Two months before Olivia's (Livi's) second birthday, our granddaughter passed away in her sleep.

She had weighed only 1lb 13oz when she was born. She had fought hard to get healthy, so this was an unexpected and heart-wrenching tragedy so many months later. After all, we were sure that she was out of the woods. Eleven months later, Peyton was born. She never made it out of the hospital, having died just four days later. For this loss to come so closely on the heels of Livi's passing was almost unbearable. These deaths nearly broke our entire family.

While we are still hurting, we have begun the healing process in the only way we could: by the grace and love of Christ.

> *"Blessed are the poor in spirit, for theirs is the kingdom of heaven. 4. Blessed are those who mourn, for they will be comforted."*
>
> — MATTHEW 5:3-4

Psalm 147:3 reads, *"He heals the brokenhearted and binds up their wounds."* And John 16:22 also reads, *"So with you: Now is your time of grief, but I will see you again and you will rejoice, and no one will take away your joy."* There is nearly an inexhaustible treasure of bible verses to look to when you are grieving—hundreds in the book of Psalms alone. In the deepest moments of my grief, I did not want to hear any of these verses. I was angry.

I kept asking myself: why would such a loving God take two beautiful babies from my daughter and us? I now realize I will probably never know why He took Livi and Peyton. As I sought after God through scripture, it dawned on me that whatever reason He took them for was ultimately to glorify Himself. And who am I to question how God is glorified?

Before he was the Apostle Paul, Saul gave shouts of approval as he held the cloaks of the men who stoned

Stephen to death. Afterwards, Acts 9:1 says, *"Saul was still breathing out murderous threats against the Lord's disciples,"* and he took great pleasure in vigorously oppressing the Christian church. His persecution was so successful that the religious leaders granted Saul's request to hunt down followers of Jesus throughout the world.

Saul aggressively sought these new believers until his dramatic conversion on the road to Damascus resulted in his abrupt religious about-face. Paul writes in Romans 8:1-2: *"Therefore, there is now no condemnation for those who are in Christ Jesus, 2. because through Christ Jesus the law of the Spirit who gives life has set you free from the law of sin and death."* The man who actively fought to crush the early church understood the truth of how our freedom is in the Lord Christ Jesus. And our guilt, if we ever deserved it in the first place, is now a thing of the past.

> *"In him we have redemption through his blood, the forgiveness of sins, in accordance with the riches of God's grace."*
>
> — EPHESIANS 1:7

Through the living sacrifice of Christ's death, we have been freely given the gifts of salvation and forgiveness of sin.

And why should this matter to you? Because you are someone who regularly sees the worst of human nature. Our profession may be doing better than expected concerning the divorce rate, but unfortunately, we far outpace every other segment of society in suicides. While the general population sees 13 out of every 100,000 people succumb to suicide, that number significantly rises to 17 out of 100,000 for law enforcement officers. In 2018, there were 167 reported law enforcement officer suicides. That number skyrocketed to a sorrowful 228 in 2019. The United States Fire Administration claims that the 103 reported firefighter suicides are only 40% of actual suicides. If this estimate is accurate, this would mean that 257 firefighters took their own lives.

While your identification as one who believes the Judeo-Christian tenets does have a positive influence in dealing with the development of suicide progression, the amount of this influence is marginal at best. You must be aware that a professing brother or sister is still susceptible to suicidal ideations. A prevailing school of thought is that years of exposure to trauma or violence makes you resilient to the effects of those events. But you know how far from the truth this statement falls. You also know how dangerous this way of thinking can be for those who are suffering mental, emotional, or spiritual distress.

> *"He has walled me in so I cannot escape; he*
> *has weighed me down with chains. 8.*
> *Even when I call out or cry for help, he*
> *shuts out my prayer."*
>
> — LAMENTATIONS 3:7-8

This is one of the clearest descriptions of the overwhelming despair Christians may find themselves in when they are contemplating suicide. The tremendous feeling of being trapped, or as Jeremiah said, *'walled me in'* is like poor Fortunato in the Edgar Allen Poe story *'The Cask of Amontillado,'* who was sealed alive in a catacomb beneath his adversary's villa. While this example is from a work of fiction, there is a real and oppressive correlation to the reality of what people experience. The inability to perform simple tasks is a physical manifestation of depression. When Jeremiah says, *'he has weighed me down with chains,'* it perfectly describes this sensation. Some describe this as 'having a concrete block on my shoes' or 'my arms are as heavy as iron bars.'

For Christians, true desperation does not come until after you feel completely abandoned by God. Although it is possible, this level of depression does not generally develop after one or two traumatic incidents. While undergoing his trials, Job certainly suffered tremendously over the course of one day. There were severe incidents stacked on top of each other, coming at him in rapid succession. I hope you have not experienced anything nearly as horrific as the trials of Job, but many of you do experience this compounding effect of one bad thing happening after another.

"Let me begin by saying God is good. He has saved me many times over, for reasons I could never understand. I simply accept that He owes me no explanation.

I was asked to share a very personal story about the day God's love protected me. Perhaps through sharing, we can find strength, courage, and humility through God's love.

I have to be honest that at the time of this incident, I was not a church-going, gospel-sharing saved soldier of God. Quite the opposite, it was possibly the darkest time of my life. I was going through a divorce. I was on a destructive path of womanizing and drinking. I was on the verge of losing my four-year-old daughter, the one last light in my life. I not only turned my back on God, I blamed Him for all my "suffrage." I questioned His very existence.

And then this happened...

Our lives as Law Enforcement Officers (LEOs) are inherently dangerous. We accept these challenges when we swear our oaths to serve and protect. On a summer day in 1996, my Tac Team was asked to support one of our detectives serve multiple felony warrants on a violent suspect known to resist arrest. Four other officers and I arrived at a location where an anonymous tip reported that our subject was located. The location was an 8-unit apartment building on a busy one-way street. We quickly set up a perimeter around the building, covering the entrance, exit routes, and as many windows as possible. After several attempts of knocking and announcing our presence at the door, we determined that we would clear the area because we could not make entry without a search warrant.

We regrouped down the block where our vehicles were all parked. We didn't really notice the time as we engaged in normal police banter. I would say approximately 20 minutes went by as we continued our conversation while we remained approximately 100 yards from the original suspect location to serve the arrest warrant. Finally, the detective said he had to leave and began to drive up the one-way street. My team and I were pretty relaxed as we began to get inside our unit to resume our patrols. Before we pulled out, the detective's voice suddenly came across the radio. He was loud and excited, he said "he's on a bike, and he's heading your way!"

Our subject apparently was inside the apartment and had waited until we cleared. He assumed that we had also left the area, but those 20 minutes we spent down the block was enough time to make him feel as though he was safe to come out. We observed our subject riding a bicycle and heading in our direction. We were traveling towards each other, as he was traveling the opposite direction on the one-way street. When he recognized that we had observed his presence and that we were preparing to deploy from our unit, he collided with our police unit. I was the first officer out of the vehicle and ran straight towards our subject. I was anticipating that he would either fight or run. As I approached, he still had the bicycle straddled between his legs. When I got approximately five feet from him, I thought I could tackle him head-on rather than go around the bicycle. This was a mistake.

I didn't anticipate that he would retreat backwards which stretched out the bicycle between us. This ended up being a terrible position for me. I had my arms stretched out in front anticipating the takedown. The bicycle was now an obstacle, which had me low and off balance. I was now about a foot from the subject but unable to reach him from this position. The next thing I remember plays out in my mind almost every day. In slow motion.

The subject retrieves a semi-automatic handgun from his waistband and aims at my head. With my outstretched arms just inches away all I could do was try to regain balance. I'm focused on the barrel, and then I hear CLICK. The subject had pulled the trigger. In a split second, but still playing out in slow motion the subject and I make eye contact. He looks at his gun and fires again. CLICK. That's two misfires at point-blank range. I drop down on my butt and begin drawing my weapon. Confused with the misfires the subject runs. We gave chase and eventually arrested the subject. The subject was shot twice but survived.

During the investigation, the subject's gun was recovered. The subject had a Russian model firearm that required 9mm Long ammunition. The subject had loaded

*9mm Short into the weapon. The chambered round was
struck, and the primer was indented but did not fire. On
this day the subject attempted to shoot me twice at point-
blank range. God blessed me with safety on this day and
many others throughout my career. He let me know that
even in my darkest days He is with me."*

— *C.C. CHARLESTON, S.C.*

Can you relate to this officer? How many times have
you suffered a horrible experience only to have another bad
situation transpire, followed by yet another bad event? Isn't
it understandable that you may get angry with God? After
all, He controls everything in the universe, right?

Job knew that the Lord was sovereign when he said to
his companions in Job 2:10, *"He replied, 'You are talking
like a foolish woman. Shall we accept good from God, and not
trouble?' In all this, Job did not sin in what he said."*

Even when he understood God's authority in everything
happening to him, Job still despaired from his utter separation
from God as we read in Job 9:16, *"Even if I summoned him
and he responded, I do not believe he would give me a hearing."*

Job did not think God would listen to him, even if he
were brought before the throne.

When you get to the point that David reached when he
wrote Psalm 55: 4-5, *"My heart is in anguish within me; the
terrors of death have fallen on me. 5. Fear and trembling
have beset me; horror has overwhelmed me"*, then you are
truly in a desperate place.

How do you come back from the edge of this deep
chasm of depression leading to potential suicidal ideation,
as dark and inviting as it may seem at the time?

*"How long, Lord? Will you forget me
forever? How long will you hide your face
from me?"*

— Psalm 13:1

Even King David suffered emotionally, and he was known as the *'man after God's own heart.'* The obvious answer is for you to take the steps necessary to ensure you never reach this point in the first place. The truth of this is that even taking all the appropriate precautions does not guarantee a successful career and life without losing hope. 1 Peter 4:12 says, *"Dear friends, do not be surprised at the fiery ordeal that has come on you to test you, as though something strange were happening to you."*

You WILL have trials. You WILL undergo suffering. But an integral part of passing through these trials is the understanding that God is sovereign over everything in existence. Knowing this reality has got to become more than simply book knowledge. Developing a spirit-acknowledged yielding to God's complete and just rule is the first step in keeping yourself from this desperation.

*"All the peoples of the earth are regarded as
nothing. He does as he pleases with the
powers of heaven and the peoples of the
earth. No one can hold back his hand or
say to him: 'What have you done?'"*

— Daniel 4:35

Who are we to question the will of God? As a

Christian, what right do you have to accuse God because of your circumstances?

You are a new creation in Christ and have His righteousness within you. You have been adopted by Him. As such, you should expect to be disciplined as any legitimate heir would be. King Solomon realized the truth behind this principle and tried to make his sons understand as well.

> *"My son, do not despise the Lord's discipline,*
> *and do not resent his rebuke, 12. because*
> *the Lord disciplines those he loves, as a*
> *father the son he delights in."*
>
> — Proverbs 3:11-12

You may be asking yourself what the good news is concerning this righteous discipline.

> *"Endure hardship as discipline; God is*
> *treating you as his children. For what*
> *children are not disciplined by their*
> *father? 8. If you are not disciplined—*
> *and everyone undergoes discipline—then*
> *you are not legitimate, not true sons and*
> *daughters at all. 9. Moreover, we have*
> *all had human fathers who disciplined*
> *us and we respected them for it. How*
> *much more should we submit to the*
> *Father of spirits and live! 10. They*
> *disciplined us for a little while as they*
> *thought best, but God disciplines us for*
> *our good, in order that we may share in*

*his holiness. 11. No discipline seems
pleasant at the time, but painful. Later
on, however, it produces a harvest of
righteousness and peace for those who
have been trained by it.”*

— Hebrews 12:7-11

Although it is difficult, disagreeable, and wildly unpleasant while you are going through it, this discipline produces a 'harvest' of peace that is waiting for you on the other side.

Getting into His word and really diving deeply into what He says to us is the second layer in your spiritual framework. The realization that circumstances do not change who you are in Christ is immensely important in maintaining your spiritual stability. Remembering that Christ died for you while you were still a sinner should help you understand the value of forgiveness through grace.

You can now give this gift of grace to others rather than the judgment and condescension that regularly accompanies the warning signs of emotional distress within the first responder field.

*“let us draw near to God with a sincere heart
and with the full assurance that faith
brings, having our hearts sprinkled to
cleanse us from a guilty conscience and
having our bodies washed with pure
water.”*

— Hebrews 10:22

Again, you cannot accomplish this through your own strength. There is only one way this happens. 2 Corinthians 5:21 says, *"God made him who had no sin to be sin for us, so that in him we might become the righteousness of God."* You are able to run to the creator of the universe and rely on Him to accomplish this work in you.

Having an active prayer life is essential in maintaining your spiritual equilibrium. Paul writes in 1 Thessalonians 5:17, *"pray without ceasing."* You are not told to do this only because of the unexpected outcomes it produces or the discipline an intentional prayer life brings but because of the personal relationship that develops between you and God. It is hurtful and immature to only go to Christ when you want something.

Have you ever known someone who only contacts you when they want something or is going through a crisis? What about a friend who keeps finding themselves in the same bad situation repeatedly, even though you have given them the advice they need to successfully move out of their calamity? Thankfully, we are not God. He does not weary of us. God has an unfathomable well of grace. Lamentations 3:22-23 reads, *"Because of the Lord's great love we are not consumed, for his compassions never fail. 23. They are new every morning; great is your faithfulness."* Or, more commonly quoted: His mercies are new every morning.

There is an inverse to this reality that is often overlooked. Because His mercy is new every morning, we should not rely on His past mercies. You are probably like a lot of Christians. You start your day looking to face the upcoming trials head-on. You keep plugging away until you can no longer push through. This is when you finally relent and turn to God and those new mercies.

What you do not realize is that taking on each day in this way is relying on these past mercies to start each day. When you start to approach each day with an eye on leaning on God from the onset, you recognize His favor much earlier in the day. Let us relate this to a daily process that is a bit more modern. You don't always wait until your computer completely runs out of battery before you charge it, do you? You ensure it has a good charge the night before, then plug it in throughout the day as needed to continue your work. Think of God's grace as the charger to your life.

You must remind yourself as often as possible of the truths of grace. Accurately grasping these truths and your freedom to engage in violence will allow you the perspective and insight to aid those around you who are suffering. Psalm 103:12 says, *"as far as the east is from the west, so far has he removed our transgressions from us."* This is why it is so important for you to understand the biblical truth of violence and trauma.

> *"fixing our eyes on Jesus, the pioneer and*
> *perfecter of faith. For the joy set before*
> *him he endured the cross, scorning its*
> *shame, and sat down at the right hand*
> *of the throne of God."*
>
> — Hebrews 12:2

When Jesus died for your sins, he did so voluntarily. He took your sin unto Himself in order to give you the gift of righteousness through grace. Remember this the next time you come across someone having a bad day. After all, you do not know what hardship someone is going through.

While you do not know the trials that others around

you may be enduring, Christ gave you the ultimate example to follow.

> *"To this you were called, because Christ*
> *suffered for you, leaving you an example,*
> *that you should follow in his steps."*
>
> — 1 Peter 2:21

This was not just the example at the cross. Christ had a lifetime of suffering. Jesus was born into a family of carpenters at a time when premarital conception was harshly punished. An unwed mother could expect community ostracization, financial, religious, and societal devastation, or even death. Jesus' family's employment and skills meant He was raised in oppressive poverty in a country and region already extremely poor.

He was the object of an infanticidal decree by the puppet king of a land ruled over by an incredibly cruel and perverse army. He was physically, emotionally, and spiritually tested by Satan. He was persecuted for showing through the prophets and scripture that He was the fulfillment of old-testament prophecy and the law.

He was betrayed by a trusted disciple and abandoned by His closest friends. Insulted, beaten, and nearly whipped to death, He was slowly suffocated in one of the most agonizing execution methods ever invented.

Through this harsh life, Jesus experienced the full range of human emotions. He had siblings, cousins, and friends.

> *"I no longer call you servants, because a*
> *servant does not know his master's*
> *business. Instead, I have called you*

*friends, for everything that I learned
from my Father I have made known to
you."*

— John 15:15

He had teachers, neighbors, and employers. There was joy. John 15:11 reads, *"I have told you this so that my joy may be in you and that your joy may be complete."* There was anger, as we read in Mark 11:15-16, *"On reaching Jerusalem, Jesus entered the temple courts and began driving out those who were buying and selling there. He overturned the tables of the money changers and the benches of those selling doves, 16. and would not allow anyone to carry merchandise through the temple courts."*

You are familiar with Jesus driving out the money changers from the temple, shouting scripture as He whipped them. This example is often used as a justification for 'righteous' anger. But let's back up just a couple of verses and see a different side of Jesus' anger.

*"The next day as they were leaving
    Bethany, Jesus was hungry. 13. Seeing
    in the distance a fig tree in leaf, he
    went to find out if it had any fruit.
    When he reached it, he found nothing
    but leaves, because it was not the season
    for figs. 14. Then he said to the tree,
    'May no one ever eat fruit from you
    again.' And his disciples heard him
    say it."*

— Mark 11:12-14

How can you not relate to that? If this was not anger, it was certainly annoyance. How many times have you had an expectation of something transpiring a certain way, been disappointed, and responded with a flash of anger? If you are anything like me, it is definitely too many times to count.

And there was sorrow.

The Bible identifies several specific times that Jesus became distraught. The timeline for these incidents roughly falls within about a week-long period. The first incident was when his very good friend Lazarus passed away. When Jesus finally arrived in Bethany, he asked where Lazarus's body had been laid, and then John 11:35, *"Jesus wept."* Just a few days later, Jesus rode the donkey down the road from the Mount of Olives Luke 19:41, *"As he approached Jerusalem and saw the city, he wept over it."*

Another example of Jesus being distraught is the night of his betrayal. In the garden, Jesus expresses his overwhelming dread when He tells the three disciples He had brought with him to pray Matthew 26:38, *"Then he said to them, 'My soul is overwhelmed with sorrow to the point of death. Stay here and keep watch with me.'"* Finally, while hanging on the cross, Matthew 27:46 says, *"About three in the afternoon Jesus cried out in a loud voice, "Eli, Eli, lema sabachthani?" (which means "My God, my God, why have you forsaken me?")."* This last example was from His complete separation from God, fulfilling the redemption of humanity.

Maybe you entered military service while still a teenager. You have witnessed violence and observed its effects. You have had to occasionally participate in acts of violence, many times finding yourself as the source of violence being used against others. Sometimes, this violence has been on an unimaginable scale. This profession takes an enormous toll on you.

Years of exposure to the harshest aspects of society can leave you feeling overwhelmed, broken, and defeated. Some of you were raised in volatile homes with an abusive or substance-addicted parent, exposing you to violence and misery from an early age. This exposure to violence and suffering from such an early age breeds a certain comfort with them; however, the loss, anxiety, feelings of uselessness, and guilt that come part and parcel with this exposure create a mental dichotomy that is difficult to subdue.

Thankfully, the bible gives you examples of how to overcome these feelings.

> *"My flesh and my heart may fail, but God is the strength of my heart and my portion forever."*
>
> — PSALM 73:26

You can follow Jesus's example. For instance, as proper as it is to mourn the loss of a dear friend, especially from combat or in the protection of others, it is not biblical to let this loss morph into a crushing gloom that overshadows every aspect of your life. I know you are familiar with John 15:13, *"Greater love has no one than this: to lay down one's life for one's friends."* But do you know what John writes in his first letter, 1 John 3:16, *"This is how we know what love is: Jesus Christ laid down his life for us. And we ought to lay down our lives for our brothers and sisters."*

It does not honor their memory or respect their sacrifice for you to languish away the remaining days of your life. This is in no way intended to minimize your grief but rather to put this grief into a proper context. Nor is this meant to substitute professional mental health treatment. Do not be afraid to seek out the help you may need. The stigmas formerly attached to such assistance have been largely refuted. Many times, it will have zero negative implications with your career and may even enhance your performance both on and off the job.

When you begin to envy those you know are doing wrong but seem to prosper, your faith, career, and personal and professional relationships can be negatively affected. One example we can reference about a righteous man beginning to question why he did the right things and suffered comes from the Old Testament. Asaph was the head of the Levites and acted as the Chief Priest during the reign of Kings David and Solomon.

It was his duty to minister before the Ark of the Covenant and enter the Most Holy Place. Look at what Asaph writes in Psalm 73:2-3, "*But as for me, my feet had almost slipped; I had nearly lost my foothold. 3. For I envied the arrogant when I saw the prosperity of the wicked.*" Asaph goes on to describe how these wicked people don't suffer from the common afflictions common to other people. Not only are they healthy and strong, they do not get sick, but they are also successful in business. These people do not just prosper; they thrive.

Verses 4-11: "*They have no struggles; their bodies are healthy and strong. 5. They are free from common human burdens; they are not plagued by human ills. 6. Therefore pride is their necklace; they clothe themselves with violence. 7. From their callous hearts comes iniquity; their evil imaginations have no limits. 8. They scoff, and speak with malice; with arrogance they threaten oppression. 9. Their mouths lay claim to heaven, and their tongues take possession of the earth. 10. Therefore their people turn to them and drink up waters in abundance. 11. They say, 'How would God know? Does the Most High know anything?'"* These people are convinced that their success is solely their own doing. They are so sure of this that they mock God in their pursuit of more. Verse 12: *"This is what the wicked are like —always free of care, they go on amassing wealth."*

They crave more: money, power, and possessions. Asaph saw this and questioned why God calls us to righteousness and why we should obey. Verses 13-16: *"Surely in vain I have kept my heart pure and have washed my hands in innocence. 14. All day long I have been afflicted, and every morning brings new punishments. 15. If I had spoken out like that, I would have betrayed your children. 16. When I tried to understand all this, it troubled me deeply."*

Can you relate to how Asaph felt? How often have you looked at the prosperous and knew in your bones that they were wicked? After wrestling with this juxtaposition for who knows how long, Asaph had an epiphany. Verses 17-19: *"till I entered the sanctuary of God; then I understood their final destiny. 18. Surely you place them on slippery ground; you cast them down to ruin. 19. How suddenly are they destroyed, completely swept away by terrors! 20. They are like a dream when one awakes; when you arise, Lord, you will despise them as fantasies."* As prosperous as these people seem, a horrific and terrifying reality awaits them. Cast to ruin, swept away by terrors, a life whose lasting value is the sum equivalent of a dream. They are just fantasies. Wow! When Asaph realizes this is the ultimate outcome of the wicked, he also understands why he was jealous of them. Verses 21-22: *"When my heart was grieved and my spirit embittered, 22. I was senseless and ignorant; I was a brute beast before you."*

Asaph takes ownership of his sin and does not attempt to deflect his perception back to God but understands that he is nothing without the help of the Lord. Verses 23-28: *"Yet I am always with you; you hold me by my right hand. 24. You guide me with your counsel, and afterward you will take me into glory. 25. Whom have I in heaven but you? And earth has nothing I desire besides you. 26. My flesh and my heart may fail, but God is the strength of my heart and my portion forever. 27. Those who are far from you will perish; you destroy all who are unfaithful to you. 28. But as for me, it is good to be near God. I have made the Sovereign Lord my refuge; I will tell of all your deeds."*

Through questioning, observation, and prayer, Asaph returned to serving the Lord. This time with a renewed love, an open heart, and a contrite spirit. David understood the ultimate fate of the wicked and Godless. Psalm 55:23, *"But you, God, will bring down the wicked into the pit of decay; the bloodthirsty and deceitful will not live out half their days. But as for me, I trust in you."* It is appropriate to question the seeming injustices we observe. But try to be more like Asaph or a David and less like a Judas.

You have been called to perform a job that has more than its fair share of hardship. James 1:2 says, *"Consider it pure joy, my brothers and sisters, whenever you face trials of many kinds."* While this verse is often cited in relation to your walk as a Christian, is it any less appropriate for your walk as a Christian first responder? There are many reasons as to why you will be faced with these trials. Regardless of the reason, the ultimate goal of these tests is to refine your faith so that you will persevere to the end. James 1:3-4, *"because you know that the testing of your faith produces perseverance. 4. Let perseverance finish its work so that you may be mature and complete, not lacking anything."*

You have been called into this profession because you are capable of experiencing the worst this life has to offer and still hug your spouse and kids when you get home. Look at what the prophet Isaiah wrote concerning God's concern for you. " Isaiah 30:10, *"Yet the Lord longs to be gracious to you; therefore, he will rise up to show you compassion. For the Lord is a God of justice. Blessed are all who wait for him!"* You are an amazing new creation in Christ. He thinks you are worthy, and so do I. Let me leave you with the truth of God's love for you. Romans 15:13 says, *"May the God of hope fill you with all joy and peace as you trust in him, so that you may overflow with hope by the power of the Holy Spirit."*

CHALLENGE COIN:

- Find a mentor, pastor, therapist, or counselor that you trust enough to discuss your personal experiences with death and violence and commitment to working through any issues that have developed.
- As much as you are able, become a mentor for a younger first responder dealing with the issues arising from death or violence.
- Dive deeply into scripture in order to research the biblical realities of why violence and death are necessary aspects of your profession. What does God say are accepted uses of violence? What are prohibited uses of violence?

CHAPTER FIVE
TRAUMA AND LOSS

"Not only so, but we also glory in our
sufferings, because we know that
suffering produces perseverance;
perseverance, character; and character,
hope."

— ROMANS 5:3-4

The physiological responses of trauma and loss manifest themselves in the same way as death and violence. Superficially, death, violence, trauma, and loss are events that would seem to have different and unique physiological responses. Yet these are so closely related that your body, brain, and psyche process all of them in the same way. The reason for this closeness of reaction lies in how your brain has been designed and its functional development.

Modern secular science says your brain evolved to release specific chemicals in response to a threat, either real or perceived. As a Christian, you know that your brain was specifically and intentionally designed by a creator. A direct result of how your brain is designed is the way in which your personality and psyche develop, as well as how your emotional personae take shape. This is accomplished through the releasing, absorption, and processing of hormones and endocrine chemicals. The way these chemical elements influence so many other aspects of what makes up who you are is why science tries to explain this away as a by-product of an evolutionary process.

God knew that living in this fallen and sinful world would be difficult.

> *"The human spirit can endure in sickness,*
> *but a crushed spirit who can bear?"*
>
> — PROVERBS 18:14

This 'crushed spirit' is experienced by everyone at some point during their life. The severity of pain created by a crushed spirit is misunderstood by people today. Do not take this the wrong way. Anxiety, depression, and the myriad of other associated conditions are real issues affecting millions of people around the world. Lamentations 3:19-20 reads, *"I remember my affliction and my wandering, the bitterness and the gall. 20. I well remember them, and my soul is downcast within me."*

HE STILL HEALS

Those who suffer from these conditions should rightly seek treatment in any way that is helpful. However, we should never forget that God is the ultimate source of spiritual and emotional relief.

*"The Lord is close to the brokenhearted and
saves those who are crushed in spirit."*

— Psalm 34:18

You know by now that the very entity who called you into this profession is also the reason that you have had to endure more hardship, suffering, and affliction than your friends who are not first responders. Conversely, the very same person who called you into the first responder community is the source of support from which you can draw an unusually deep well of strength.

There are many layers of loss. Loss of a loved one, status, or job are some of the common ones that first responders face. The loss of your dignity following the revelation of bad or immoral choices is a reality that all first responders face, even those who claim faith in Christ. Look at this example from a Federal Agent deployed to New Orleans during the Hurricane Katrina disaster and how the loss of an entire community affected him.

"In the summer of 2005, I was working for a highly mobile Federal Agency tasked with counter-terrorism and the protection of civil aviation, stationed in South Florida. I was assigned to the training department as an instructor and, as such, I was not in the regular flying schedule and was available for special deployments. In August, Hurricane Katrina made landfall in New Orleans, Louisiana. It quickly became apparent that the destruction and chaos were on a scale that has rarely been seen in the United States and would require an all hands on deck response from the federal government. A few days after the storm had passed through, we received the call advising us

that my federal agency would be sending a contingent of personnel in to secure the New Orleans airport, establish screening checkpoints, and provide security onboard all flights out. The airport needed to be reopened as soon as possible to help evacuate the people who were gathering there.

Many of these residents had lost everything that they owned and were just looking for a way out. They were sick, hungry, and frightened. Society had broken down in New Orleans, and people could not get the food, water, medicine, or shelter that they needed to survive. We arrived into this chaos and immediately began to restore order and bring about a workable solution for screening passengers before they boarded the flights out. The electricity was inoperable region-wide, and many people were living temporarily inside of the airport. There was no trash pickup or sanitation services available, so the situation was quickly becoming critical as the trash and filth accumulated. I was a fairly seasoned law enforcement officer, but what I witnessed there was overwhelming to me. I'd never even considered that the United States could become a third-world country, but I was witnessing that very thing with my own eyes. One natural disaster could reduce a modern American city to utter ruin overnight. I was truly shaken by what I saw, and in some of the few, quiet moments that I had I began to wonder where God was in all of this destruction and death.

His answer was not long in coming. He did not speak audibly, but He couldn't have been more clear if He had spoken to me out of a burning bush. I was patrolling an area outside of the security checkpoint when I came across an elderly African-American woman who had found a broom somewhere and had taken the initiative to start sweeping out a clean spot in the sea of trash. No one told her to do it, she just knew that it needed to be done so she did it. In that instant, I knew that God was showing me that He was there, a light in the darkness, illustrated by this one woman's selfless act. It wasn't much, but it showed me that one person can make a difference and God is showing us the hope that's just beyond the veil that our human eyes can see. He's there in all of our tragedies and triumphs. He's there with us every day loving us and calling us to be His light in this present darkness.

Overwhelmed by God's goodness and His love, I quietly approached this wonderful living example of Christ-like behavior and gently placed my hand on her shoulder. I spoke the only words that I could muster through my emotions, 'thank you.' She merely smiled and kept working. That day, so long ago, still comes back to me when I wonder where God is in situations that arise in my life and I'm reminded that He's always here, ready to love, encourage, and empower me to do whatever He has called me to do. I'm humbled when I realize that the God of the universe would take the time to answer the question of His child when he calls. I know that if I can trust Him to hear me when I call, then I can be sure that He'll be faithful no matter what comes my way."

— *J.S.~ Miami, FL*

God created you with all the abilities you will ever need to excel as a first responder. Yet He knew that you would need comfort and relief from the very experiences He has called you to endure. Many passages in scripture compare God to a caring and protective shepherd caring for and seeking the good of His flock.

"He will cover you with his feathers, and
under his wings you will find refuge; his
faithfulness will be your shield and
rampart. 5. You will not fear the terror
of night, nor the arrow that flies by day,
6. nor the pestilence that stalks in the
darkness, nor the plague that destroys at
midday."

— PSALM 91:4-6

How timely is this passage, particularly verse 6? I predict that the ripple effects associated with the reactions to the COVID-19 virus will continue to be felt for years if not decades.

SOME MEMORIES NEVER FADE

The trauma you experience as a first responder becomes a part of your makeup. Those horrific fatal teenager accident scenes, domestic violence victims, sudden and unexplained child deaths, and sexual trauma victims release endorphins, hormones, and other chemicals that create a surplus of residual brain reactions. It is inevitable that these brain chemicals build up and begin to physically change the surface shape of your brain as the years go on.

No matter what you have experienced, or how your prior traumatic familiarity was earned, this is an unavoidable reality of your physical design. And this change in brain topography continues to occur. Sorry to break it to you, but this means you will never reach a level of adeptness where you will no longer be affected by traumatic incidents.

Just as the physiologic reaction to trauma and loss

mimics those of death and violence, so too does the emotional reaction. The cumulative consequences of these traumatic experiences and incidents of loss build into a seemingly insurmountable obstacle.

Unfortunately, the first responder community has historically viewed this aggregate emotional accumulation from trauma and loss as something to be of a less than equal significance than those emotions from death and violence. Particularly from violence in which you are personally involved. While this outdated and irresponsible attitude has begun to shift, the change has not occurred quickly enough or been acceptably widespread. Luckily, there are two sources of solace to which you have immediate and unlimited access to two sources of solace.

> *"Then they cried to the Lord in their trouble,*
> *and he saved them from their distress.*
> *14. He brought them out of darkness, the*
> *utter darkness, and broke away their*
> *chains."*
>
> — Psalm 107:13-14

As a Christian, you have unfettered access to God through prayer and the scriptures. Christianity is the only major world religion where this unfettered access can be found. Every single other religion requires some sort of ceremonial rite before the believer can approach their deity.

Because of this immediate access to Jesus, you have the ability to literally cry out whenever your burden becomes too heavy.

ENCOUNTERING THE COMFORTER

The Psalms are full of examples of people suffering through devastating spiritual unrest and anxiety. Regularly reading the Psalms can be helpful at any time, but is especially so during those dark times when your emotional burden becomes devastating. Psalm 145:18-19 says, *"The Lord is near to all who call on him, to all who call on him in truth. 19. He fulfills the desires of those who fear him; he hears their cry and saves them."*

God wants to carry the heavy burden created by your constant exposure to trauma.

> *"So do not fear, for I am with you; do not be dismayed, for I am your God. I will strengthen you and help you; I will uphold you with my righteous right hand."*
>
> — ISAIAH 41:10

God has given you the ability to lay your burden down any time you choose. 1 Peter 5:7 says, *"Cast all your anxiety on him because he cares for you."* There is no doubt that God cares for you and is intimately concerned with your well-being.

Any deficiency or lack of compassion for the burden you carry is completely and solely the responsibility of one person: you. Isaiah 54:10 says, *"Though the mountains be shaken and the hills be removed, yet my unfailing love for you will not be shaken nor my covenant of peace be removed,' says the Lord, who has compassion on you."* The Lord never fails. As hard as this may be to hear, I would be remiss to overlook such an important truth simply because it is difficult and potentially offensive. Any breakdown of communication, communion, and relationship with Jesus is your fault.

A Journey Worth Taking

Go with me on an analogous journey, if you will. Think of it like this: What do you think would happen to you if you had to carry an explosive device from the first-class section of an aircraft all the way back to the rear galley? According to the action-packed blockbuster movie '*Non-Stop,*' this is a potentiality faced by the dedicated men and women of the Federal Air Marshal Service every time they board an aircraft. How would you feel carrying this device just a few feet, let alone a hundred and fifty feet? I think you would agree that your stress level would be off the charts.

Your blood pressure and heart rate would skyrocket. You would be sweating profusely, affecting your handling of the device. More than likely, your arms would feel heavy, and your legs like they are wrapped in lead. Now imagine that two seats away is a brand new, fully functional bomb-suit, tailor-made just for you. Would you want to put it on before handling the explosive? Now, let's say, five rows away is a top-of-the-line explosive handling robot. This isn't just any run-of-the-mill robot. This robot is operated by a wireless controller that just so happens to be configured in the same design as your favorite gaming system controller. Oh, and it has an operating range of 1,000 meters.

Would you start to feel more confident having to handle the device, even if it was just a small margin of comfort? Suppose now that you discover there is an explosive containment chamber in the back of the aircraft where you can deposit the device and render it safe as opposed to whatever you would have done with it previously. How would you perceive this situation, and what might your stress levels be given this new understanding of the circumstances? Even if you are not a trained Explosives Ordnance Disposal Technician, you would likely be confident, if not comfortable, in your chances of surviving the incident. Now imagine, if you will: go back to the beginning of this analogy. You see the device. Your very first reaction after your gut drops is to immediately ask God to help and protect you. You look over and see the suit but say to yourself, "*Nah, I got this.*" You pick up the explosive, and you get on the move.

As you walk toward the back of the plane, you ask God to deliver you from your situation for at least the second time when you come across the robot. You say to yourself, "*I'm still doing good. But, cool robot. It kinda looks like Wall-e.*" As you continue to walk, you see the explosive containment chamber and say, "*I think it would be better to put this in the lavatory. After all, the door has a lock.*" To any sane person this sounds like insanity, right? Well, this is exactly what you do when you refuse to allow God to carry your burdens. All the resources needed to ease your anxiety and increase your chance of making it through the hard situation have been provided. They are readily available and accessible. They are sitting right there. Yet, you chose not to utilize them.

What then can you do? What steps can you take to repair this damaged condition that has developed between you and Christ? Psalm 30:2-3 says, "*Lord my God, I called to you for help, and you healed me. 3. You, Lord, brought me up from the realm of the dead; you spared me from going down to the pit.*" Running back into the arms of the Lord is the surest way to repair this relationship. Psalm 34:4 says, "*I sought the Lord, and he answered me; he delivered me from all my fears.*" Seek Him and accept the comfort He gives.

As a Christian, you are not granted the luxury of an unspoiled, idyllic, trauma-free life. Jesus says in Matthew 10:22a, "*You will be hated by everyone because of me,*" and Paul writes in 2 Timothy 3:12, "*In fact, everyone who wants to live a godly life in Christ Jesus will be persecuted.*" As a first responder, this truth is magnified tenfold. But this does not mean that you must be hunched over by the heavy burden you carry around like a badge of honor, either.

> "*Yet this I call to mind and therefore I have hope: 22. Because of the Lord's great love we are not consumed, for his compassions never fail. 23. They are new every morning; great is your faithfulness.*"
>
> — LAMENTATION 3:21-23

His mercy and faithfulness are new every morning. There are a myriad of secondary benefits that you will begin to receive once you are finally able to lay your burden on Christ. Some of these benefits manifest by improving physical responses that can demonstrate lowered blood pressure, reduced heart rate, and improved stress levels. The benefits may also manifest in a clarity of thinking and calmness under pressure. Or you may notice an improvement in professional and personal interpersonal interactions.

One of the most satisfying, though, is when you are able to help others through their own difficult trials. Let's look at this example of a Christian first responder who helps a victim of human trafficking, a unique crime that involves the loss of self.

> *"One of the stories I have about being a Christian responder is helping a young migrant woman escape the cycle of trafficking. While on uniformed duty at an international airport, I noticed several signs that this woman was the victim of human trafficking. She had landed at this international airport without a dollar to her name, no cell phone, and had been able to separate from an abusive male.*
>
> *My partner and I were able to find a woman's shelter in the State that could assist her. Further, we were able to provide transportation fees and escorted her to a Greyhound Station where she could get to the women's shelter. We also arranged for shelter staff to pick her up on the other end.*
>
> *It would have been easier to do 'the minimum.' And, unfortunately, there are all too many that have the habit of looking the other way to avoid trouble. In this case, my Christian beliefs made me take some extra steps to help a vulnerable neighbor in need."*
>
> — *S.S. MAUI, HI*

Getting through your struggle and coming out the other side provides you with a new perspective.

> *"Praise be to the God and Father of our*
> *Lord Jesus Christ, the Father of*
> *compassion and the God of all comfort,*
> *4. who comforts us in all our troubles, so*
> *that we can comfort those in any trouble*

with the comfort we ourselves receive
from God."

— 2 Corinthians 1:3-4

You are no longer simply sympathetic to those going through difficult times but are now able to have empathy for others going through a similar trial.

You have been there. You have walked that fractured path and found your way through.

"Even though I walk through the valley of the
shadow of death, I will fear no evil, for
you are with me; your rod and your staff,
they comfort me."

— Psalm 23:4 (ESV)

God has designed this for our benefit. One of the greatest earthly supports we have is the ability to seek guidance from someone who has gone through a similar hardship to what we are experiencing. This is the root foundation on which Alcoholics Anonymous and similar programs are built.

As these self-help programs can attest, 'sponsors' are essential for an addict's recovery. The same principle holds true for spiritual recovery. While this topic deals with spiritual distress from trauma and loss, the journey looks similar to addiction recovery. You suffer from a trauma that rends your spirit. You are wounded but initially ignore the wound as you stoically press on. As it begins to heal, the wound creates a scar. Sometimes, this scar settles and is less onerous. Sometimes, it becomes more irritating. This pattern continues until you are unable to deal with all the spiritual scarring and are at your wit's end. This is the crucial moment when help can come from someone who has gone through a similar experience.

There is a uniqueness that is born from a relationship that occurs when you willingly submit to supporting others in their time of need. You understand the weaknesses that come from spiritual warfare. You can guide and encourage this individual, secure in the knowledge that you have trod the very ground they are stepping on. You are like a spiritual point man who has broken new ground on the trial, which they can now follow. This is an earthly expression of what Christ has done for you. Isaiah 51:12a, "*I, even I, am he who comforts you.*"

When you call on the Lord in your time of trouble, He will answer. Psalm 55:22 says, "*Cast your cares on the Lord and he will sustain you; he will never let the righteous be shaken.*" The Lord is the ultimate sanctuary in your time of trouble.

> "*From the ends of the earth I call to you, I*
> *call as my heart grows faint; lead me to*
> *the rock that is higher than I. 3. For you*
> *have been my refuge, a strong tower*
> *against the foe.*"
>
> — PSALM 61: 2-3

He is the ultimate port in the storm. He is the definitive stronghold in which to find solace.

> "*Yes, my soul, find rest in God; my hope*
> *comes from him. 6. Truly he is my rock*

*and my salvation; he is my fortress, I will
not be shaken. 7. My salvation and my
honor depend on God; he is my mighty
rock, my refuge."*

— Psalm 62: 5-7

How awesome a responsibility it is to be the lighthouse that helps guide the ship from danger! How awesome is it that you are that lighthouse through your relationship with Jesus Christ? You are not just a first responder but a beacon of love and hope, tearing through the storm clouds blowing in someone else's life.

You have been called to a high and exalted mission. This should be a sobering realization for many, not a prideful boast. The only way you will be able to fulfill this mission in the way you are called is by a submissiveness of spirit.

*"For this is what the high and exalted One
        says—he who lives forever, whose name is
        holy: 'I live in a high and holy place, but
        also with the one who is contrite and
        lowly in spirit, to revive the spirit of the
        lowly and to revive the heart of the
        contrite.'"*

— Isaiah 57:15

When you are truly contrite of heart, it pleases God, as we read in Psalm 30:2-3: *"Lord my God, I called to you for help, and you healed me. 3. You, Lord, brought me up from the realm of the dead; you spared me from going down to the pit."*

David relied on God to see him through difficult times, but he also had friends with whom he could confide and lean on. Jonathon was closer to David than his own biological brothers. Jonathon was a Godly man and constant support for David in his early life. Up until his dying day, Jonathon defied his father Saul on issues where he felt God recognizing David as the anointed King of Israel.

Later, David had the prophet Nathan to be a guide and counselor. It was Nathan who revealed David's sinfulness with the whole Bathsheba-Uriah-adultery-murder business (a glaring and blatant example of violence that is not condoned by the bible).

Once Nathan confronted him with the sins he had committed, David could no longer deceive himself or justify his actions as being honorable, necessary, or pure. David immediately broke and begged God for forgiveness. Psalm 51:17, "*My sacrifice, O God, is a broken spirit; a broken and contrite heart you, God, will not despise.*" David understood that as bad and traumatic as his actions were toward other people, he had sinned against God and God alone. This is similar to what happens when a perpetrator commits a crime.

Not only does the offender violate another person either directly (crime against a person) or indirectly (crime against property), but they also violate the laws of the land (municipality, state, federal, etc.) As such, the governing body has the final say in prosecution, even if doing so goes against the wishes of the victim.

Honestly, how many times have you responded to a call-for-service only to have the victim begging you not to arrest the one who committed the crime? Think about all the domestic violence incidents. The authority from which the crime occurs is not a contractual exchange from person to person. It is derived from a higher authority than all of the parties involved. Or at least that is how it is supposed to work.

RESISTING HIS CONVICTION

Every single one of us is capable of terrible things.

> *"The acts of the flesh are obvious: sexual immorality, impurity and debauchery; 20. idolatry and witchcraft; hatred, discord, jealousy, fits of rage, selfish ambition, dissensions, factions 21. and envy; drunkenness, orgies, and the like. I warn you, as I did before, that those who live like this will not inherit the kingdom of God."*
>
> — GALATIANS 5:19-21

Even Paul, the greatest evangelical missionary in the history of the world, struggled with his sinful nature.

Romans 7:14-20 says, *"We know that the law is spiritual; but I am unspiritual, sold as a slave to sin. 15. I do not understand what I do. For what I want to do I do not do, but what I hate I do. 16. And if I do what I do not want to do, I agree that the law is good. 17. As it is, it is no longer I myself who do it, but it is sin living in me. 18. For I know that good itself does not dwell in me, that is, in my sinful nature. For I have the desire to do what is good, but I cannot carry it out. 19. For I do not do the good I want to do, but the evil I do not want to do—this I keep on doing. 20. Now if I do* *what I do not want to do, it is no longer I who do it, but <u>it is</u> <u>sin living in me</u> that does it."*

So, too, you are not exempt from this potentiality based on your status as a Christian, Police Officer, Firefighter, Attorney, Emergency Medical Technician, Missionary, Corrections Officer, Nurse, Doctor, member of the Military, Veteran, or first responder of any kind. We have seen this time and again throughout history. Angel of Death nurses, serial rapist law enforcement officers, missionaries turned pornographic filmmakers and stars. Shoot! One of, if not the first, designated serial killer to be recognized in the United States was a physician named Dr. H.H. Holmes. He was a surgeon who terrorized Chicago by murdering at least 34 people, with estimates as high as 200 victims. You and I know these examples are anomalies and far from the norm. These cases do not even represent the outliers of the brave and honorable men and women working in the armed forces and first responder field. However, they are provided with the sole purpose of reminding you of the level of depravity to which any person is capable of sinking.

While you have not reached the level exhibited by these examples, it is safe to say that you have fallen short of God's requirements as we read in Romans 3:23, *"for all have sinned and fall short of the glory of God."*

> *"For whoever keeps the whole law and yet*
> *stumbles at just one point is guilty of*
> *breaking all of it."*
>
> — JAMES 2:10

This is when you get annoyed and lash out at the

person after the fifth time they have called to report something that ended up being false just because they wanted someone with whom to talk. This does not seem like such a bad example, right?

After all, Jesus yelled at and even whipped the money changers in the temple. But... Jesus quoted scripture at them as to reason why what they were doing was wrong. He did not call the money changers "Idiot," "Stupid," "Time-waster," or other derogatory things based on them as an individual.

> *"But I tell you that anyone who is angry with a brother or sister will be subject to judgment. Again, anyone who says to a brother or sister, 'Raca,' is answerable to the court. And anyone who says, 'You fool!' will be in danger of the fire of hell."*
>
> — MATTHEW 5:22

You cannot help it. Sin is so innately ingrained into your very fiber that you were completely unaware of it when left to our own righteousness. Psalm 51:5, *"Surely I was sinful at birth, sinful from the time my mother conceived me."*

You are unable to stop your sinful nature by your own strength or force of will. One such avenue of relief that is available to you, which is blocked to the unsaved person, is the ability to approach the throne of God. The author of Hebrews understood this. Look at what they wrote in Hebrews 4:16, *"Let us then approach God's throne of grace with confidence, so that we may receive mercy and find grace to help us in our time of need."* David was another person who understood the truth of this concept quite intimately.

There may come a day when you will have to inflict trauma upon another person. This may be in your official capacity or during your off-duty hours. You may have already experienced this, maybe even several times. Understanding that the appropriate application of trauma is biblical and proper. There may also come a time when you find within yourself that you have reached your limit for trauma. Or maybe you realize that you may have engaged in an unbiblical application of trauma.

If this later is true, you are not alone.

Seek forgiveness and refuge in the Lord. The entirety of Psalm 51 is a passionate plea for forgiveness.

> *"Have mercy on me, O God, according to*
> *your unfailing love; according to your*
> *great compassion blot out my*
> *transgressions. 2. Wash away all my*
> *iniquity and cleanse me from my sin."*
>
> — PSALM 51:1-2

You are in a tough profession. The majority of people in our society refuse to place themselves in the situations you find yourself in on a regular basis. Seeing the worst of humanity and being witness to another person's very worst day takes an incredible toll on everyone involved. You are doing an amazing job. Keep doing it. You are a warrior in the truest sense of the word.

Challenge Coin:

- Read Psalm 51 in its entirety. Open up to your accountability partner regarding feelings of anger or frustration with aspects of the job that can creep up and affect your normal judgment while on the job. Pray about these as often as possible.
- Research biblical passages that ordain your role as someone who may have to inflict trauma. Delineate between biblical uses of violence and those that are not. Discuss these verses with at least two other Christian first responders in your circle of influence.
- Identify a younger coworker who seems to be struggling with their role in having to parcel out trauma. As much as you are able, prayerfully mentor this individual.

Chapter Six
Making An Impact

"Remember this: Whoever turns a sinner
from the error of their way will save
them from death and cover over a
multitude of sins."

— James 5:20

Many times it is believed that grandiose gestures, heroic actions, or some other selfless act are the best way to make an impact as a Christian first responder. Luckily, nothing could be farther from the truth.

Making an impact is wholly dependent on your attitude towards Christ, your fellow believers, and the lost whom you encounter daily. You may think this may be harder than saving a family from a burning building or jumping into your bunker gear and sliding down that iconic pole.

While you are more than able to make a lasting impact relying on your own strength, capabilities, and efforts, these are totally dependent on things within your sphere of influence and control. Your focus becomes more and more internal.

> *"No one should seek their own good, but the*
> *good of others."*
>
> — 1 Corinthians 10:24

Your successes of impactful activity elevate impressions of self-importance, while your inability to make or sustain an impact will deflate your feelings of importance. This is not what Solomon meant when he wrote Proverbs 11:25, "*A generous person will prosper; whoever refreshes others will be refreshed.*" Your attitude towards Jesus Christ is the ultimate deciding factor in how you can impact those around you.

"Several years ago, I was a Sergeant on our agency's street crimes team. Since we were with the county Sheriff's Office, we would help local PDs by patrolling high-crime areas of all the cities in the county. Most of us, including myself, were also part of our SWAT team. As a Sergeant, I would always pray for protection for myself and my team, but would also pray that my actions and decisions would be morally and legally correct. I also prayed that I would not jeopardize my deputies or the citizens of the community with my decisions and actions.

Late one Saturday night, my partner (a deputy) and I were patrolling a known gang area in one of our cities. Our shift was almost over, and we were getting ready to head back to the station. We heard a call go out on our scanner about a suspicious subject at a strip mall, possibly trying to break into some of the closed businesses. They put out a description of the subject and an address for the mall.

We realized we were just coming up on the strip mall. As we pulled into the parking lot, we saw a subject matching the description walking across the parking lot. He was walking in our direction so we stopped, shined our spotlights on him, and told him to walk towards us. My partner was driving, and I was on the passenger side of our unit. As my partner radioed our dispatch of our stop and requested the local PD to respond, I had the subject walk toward my side of the car.

As he was walking toward me, I noticed the tip of what looked like a revolver handle sticking out of the top of his right front pocket. As I drew my pistol, I told my partner the subject possibly had a gun in his pocket. My partner drew his pistol, and we were both pointing our guns at him, but my partner later told me he could not see the subject's pockets due to him being on the other side of our unit. The subject must have heard me tell my partner about the gun because he told us it wasn't real and started to reach for it.

We both yelled at him to stop and put his hands up. The subject complied, put his hands up, but then said again it wasn't real. He started to reach down to his pocket again, and we yelled again for him to stop and put his hands up. Looking back, I remembered the confused look on the subject's face as he slowly raised his hands back up. We told him to keep his hands up and not to reach for the gun again, or we might shoot him.

Again, he looked confused, told us it was a toy cap pistol, and started to reach for it again. For a third time, we yelled at him to stop, put his hands up, and not reach for the gun. Additionally, each time he reached for the gun, he got closer to pulling it out, and we were both ready to shoot him (as my partner later told me). The subject finally complied, kept his hands raised, and did exactly as we told him as we secured him without any further incident.

After handcuffing him, we pulled out two toy cap pistols from his right front pocket and a flashlight from his left front pocket. As we talked with him, I initially thought he might be under the influence of drugs or alcohol, but realized he might have a disability. As I talked to him more, I was able to determine he was developmentally disabled. When the local PD arrived, they instantly recognized the subject as a local man, who is developmentally disabled, but loves law enforcement. They said he thinks of himself as a cop and likes to make sure the local businesses are secure. When we told them what happened, they were obviously concerned and said they would return him to his house and speak with his caregiver.

I remember when we returned to our unit, and just sat for a moment in silence, thinking about how close we came to shooting the subject, and how devastating it would have been. I don't remember praying during the incident, it happened so quickly. But I know the Lord was with me and helped protect that young man. I kept thinking about what would have happened if we had shot him - the pain it would have afflicted on so many. It also hit me hard because my older brother was autistic and I have a soft spot in my heart for the developmentally disabled. I believe the Lord put it on that young man's mind to finally listen and not reach for the gun; I believe He guided us in being patient, in being under control, and reminded us of our training.

Over the years, I've seen lesser-threat incidents turn deadly. I remember thanking the Lord for protecting the young man, and for protecting me and my partner. The *incident would haunt me from time to time, thinking about what would have happened if I had shot him. But, as a Christian, I was able to go to God and remember His goodness, His provision, and His sovereignty over the whole situation. The Lord is my comfort and my rock!"*

— *D.L. VENTURA, CA*

Again, I am sure you can relate many similar stories to this. What I find interesting from this story is that while this deputy did not have time to actively pray during this kinetic incident, they had developed an intentional prayer life in conjunction with their work life. The years of specific prayers guided their actions, thoughts, and post-incident analysis.

This is the synthesis of what happens when you balance your physical fitness and spiritual training. They become compliments to each other and a springboard to making a lasting impact on everyone around you. Exactly as this deputy had done for years.

IMPACT THROUGH SERVICE

How, then, do you become an inspiration to others and make an impact without impressive exploits or relying on your own strength? The simple answer is: You must focus on Christ and seek his glory. I say simple, but you know just how difficult this can be for A-Type, Alpha first responders by now.

You are used to responding to horrendous scenes where an untold number of people are looking to you for direction, inspiration, and assurance. The resultant adrenaline dump can have a narcotic-like effect on the brain that can lead you to crave it like a drug. This effect is very much the same as what extreme athletes experience, which drives them to continually seek greater and greater risk.

Lucky for you, the more you rely on Christ as the source of your encouragement, the more generous He is in providing for you when the time arises.

"I grew up in a Christian home. I accepted the Lord in the 7th grade. I grew up in the suburbs of NY, and I wanted for nothing. I wanted to be a veterinarian my whole life until I went into the 10th grade and the Law Enforcement Explorers Program came to our police department. I joined them without hesitation and soon became the president. There was a stirring within me that seemed that I needed more. I was being groomed to become a police officer within my hometown of White Plains, NY and once I became of age it was a guarantee.

In my senior year, I didn't want to wait until I was 21 to become a police officer. I needed something to occupy me until that time and I did not want to go to college at that time. I went to an Air Force recruiter and took the ASVAB on a whim and scored relatively high. I had a choice of whatever I wanted, but I had to wait for over a year to go into the service, and the job I chose wasn't guaranteed.

I remember voicing my displeasure with the recruiter and the Army recruiter overheard me. He called me over and guaranteed my job, where I was going to be stationed, and when. I swore in at the office, which was the first declaration of intent, and was given a packet. I stopped by the police department, but the detectives weren't in the office. I left the packet in the office by mistake. Looking back, I totally forgot the obligation altogether.

That evening I received a call from the youth detectives

telling me to report to the station after school the next day. They asked a lot of questions and started telling me not to go into the Army and that my future was with the police department. In some way, my youthful rebellion and angst fueled me to go into the Army even more!

In the Army, I passed everything, got promoted, got married, and had a son. I remember thinking that my life would be complete once I had a house, a husband, and 2.5 kids...whatever that means! I served honorably and got out to be a wife and Army mom. While I was living in Germany my parents called and mentioned that the police department was hiring. I flew back home and took the test. I ended up staying in NY and became an EMT working on the city's emergency ambulance.

I became a federal police officer in NYC protecting federal buildings, employees, and prisoners. I moved up the ranks and then took a job in upstate NY just before 9/11. I was activated and deployed to Ground Zero with the NYNG for four months. When I returned, I was a changed woman. I no longer had peace in what I was doing. I wanted to serve my country on a more tangible level. I thought about joining the Federal Air Marshal Service for about 1 year and then applied. It was no time before I was contacted and hired.

I write all of this to tell you of the day that I truly felt accepted and justified in my position. When you serve in the military, you have an unending obligation to feel deserving of the uniform. It carries with you throughout the course of your life, and it can be damaging if it isn't put in its proper place. I sustained a few injuries in the military and in EMS. By the time I obtained a position with the DHS, I was struggling to feel "worthy" of the position.

While at work, I remember reading a devotional from

Dr. Charles Stanley. In the devotional, he stated that where you are is EXACTLY where the LORD wants you to be. I remember feeling unworthy of the responsibility in which He had placed me. After reading this devotional I thought to the LORD, "How am I deserving of the position you have me in LORD?" He answered me right away! He took me to 1 Thessalonians 5:14-15 (NASB), which states '14. We urge you, brothers and sisters, admonish the unruly, encourage the fainthearted, help the weak, be patient with everyone. 15. See that no one repays another with evil for evil, but always seek what is good for one another and for all people.' I knew this verse applied to the Body of Christ, but the Holy Spirit spoke to me and let me know that this is how I am to serve others with my position in Him.

From that day forward, I never felt undeserving of where the LORD has placed me! He also led me to Colossians 3:23 (NASB) which states, 'Whatever you do, do your work heartily, as for the Lord and not for people.' This taught me that as long as I filter everything through the LORD, I am able to accomplish everything he asks of me. It was not easy to not look for the approval of man, but this kept me grounded and still does to this day.

No matter where your life takes you, we all come to the question in our lives if this is where we were meant to be. Whether you are a janitor or a CEO, we all come to this realization in our lives. I know for sure that without the Lord in my life, I would still be searching for the answer. Thank you, Jesus, for your love, compassion, and mercy! Thank you for the helper who has sustained me in my life! Amen"

— M.K. Houston, TX

I am impressed by how this first responder describes their journey. This story spans a literal lifetime of service to realize the impact they have been able to have. First responders have a hard time with waiting. You want to find, figure out, attack, and fix the problems that arise in your scope of influence. When we are forced to wait, our self-driven motivation is exposed. This selfish exposure results in angst in the soul.

> *"The Lord is good to those whose hope is in him, to the one who seeks him; it is good to wait quietly for the salvation of the Lord."*
>
> — LAMENTATIONS 3:25-26

Once you understand the truth of this verse, you realize the good news. While you may be forced to wait, you do not have to wait passively.

PURSUING THE GREAT SHEPHERD

When you seek Him, you are actively pursuing Him through prayer and diving into the scripture. This searching for God readjusts your focus from the impact you can have through your own strength to that which the Lord can accomplish.

This also holds true for the struggles you face. How much more of an impact do you think you can have by waiting for the Lord to accomplish His goals? I know it is hard to submit to this waiting, especially as Alpha first responders. But this is exactly what you have willingly signed on for as a follower of Christ.

Pay close attention to what the Psalmist is saying in Psalm 119:105-112:

> Your word is a lamp for my feet,
>   a light on my path.
> 106
> I have taken an oath and confirmed it,
>   that I will follow your righteous laws.
> 107
> I have suffered much;
>   preserve my life, Lord, according to your
>   word.
> 108
> Accept, Lord, the willing praise of my mouth,
>   and teach me your laws.
> 109
> Though I constantly take my life in my
>   hands,
>   I will not forget your law.
> 110
> The wicked have set a snare for me,
>   but I have not strayed from your precepts.
> 111
> Your statutes are my heritage forever;
>   they are the joy of my heart.
> 112
> My heart is set on keeping your decrees
>   to the very end.

The modern-day first responder parallels stick out like a sore thumb. Verse 106: '*I have taken an oath and confirmed it, that I will follow your righteous laws.*' Which of you reading has not taken an oath, either for their current position, military service, or both? Verse 107: '*I have suffered much; preserve my life.*' Every single person I have ever met in the first responder field has suffered much. Who among you has never pleaded with God to preserve their life at least once in this profession? A profound insight is found in verse '109: *Though I constantly take my life in my hands, I will not forget your law.*' This is the epitome of what you do every day. And not just the law enforcement officers out there. Doctors, nurses, dispatchers, firefighters, paramedics, E.M.T.s, and even pastors and missionaries are bound to uphold the law in the pursuit of their duties. The most insightful perspective as it relates to the modern first responder community is found in verse '110: *<u>The wicked have set a snare for me</u>, but I have not strayed from your precepts.*' (emphasis added)

Even when being attacked, ambushed, and having people set traps in order to catch the psalmist unawares, he never strayed from the precepts set forth in God's word.

How is the Psalmist able to go through all of these different trials and still constantly take his life into his hands? Verse 105: '*Your word is a lamp for my feet, a light on my path.*' By studying God's word, that's how. By immersing himself in scripture, contemplation, memorization, and thoughtful consideration the psalmist is able to recognize the only way he is able to walk the path set before him is by studying the scriptures. Verse 108:' *Accept, Lord, the willing praise of my mouth, and teach me your laws.*' The author knew that the only way to truly praise the Lord is by asking that your worship be acceptable by HIS standards and not your own. One of the best ways to ensure you are seeking God's heart is to know God's laws, i.e.: the scripture. Verse 111, '*Your statutes are my heritage forever;*

they are the joy of my heart.' The joy derived from continual and regularly appointed time in God's word is the only way to find true and lasting joy in this world. 112. *'My heart is set on keeping your decrees to the very end.'* The psalmist knew the pursuit of God's heart would be a lifelong undertaking. When you seek after God, there will never be a moment where you have 'arrived.' This biblical immersion is something that should be a passion of yours that lasts until your final day on this earth.

An Unending Hope

There is an everlasting source of encouragement when you begin to focus on doing good for others as a submission to Christ Jesus and not to glorify yourself. Psalm 37:4-6 says, *"Take delight in the Lord, and he will give you the desires of your heart. 5. Commit your way to the Lord; trust in him, and he will do this: 6. He will make your righteous reward shine like the dawn, your vindication like the noonday sun."* Christ will glorify Himself through your submission to his will. He will turn this obedience into something that no one around you will be able to ignore. He will make your impact a thing that everyone will be able to recognize as something special.

When you focus on Christ and his glory, it frees you from the burden of having to be the source of inspiration for those around you.

> *"Therefore encourage one another and build each other up, just as in fact you are doing."*
>
> — 1 Thessalonians 5:11

You will be seen as an encouragement to so many different groups within your sphere of influence.

> *"And do not forget to do good and to share*
> *with others, for with such sacrifices God is*
> *pleased."*

— Hebrews 13:16

Family members, coworkers (both subordinates and superiors), criminals, victims, witnesses, and non-first responder friends will be affected by this change of focus toward Christ and His will.

When you do good for others for His glory it pleases God.

> *"And do not forget to do good and to share*
> *with others, for with such sacrifices God is*
> *pleased."*

— Hebrews 13:16

It does not diminish your authority as a law enforcement officer to be respectful to your arrestee. Does it take away from your ability as a medical provider to show respect to that 'frequent flyer' who is generally a nuisance? Of course not.

> *"So in everything, do to others what you*
> *would have them do to you, for this sums*
> *up the Law and the Prophets."*

— Matthew 7:12

When you can do this for no other purpose than to glorify God, you will see your impact grow exponentially.

Carry Each Other's Burdens

One of the greatest benefits to occur from taking upon yourself a portion of the burden with your brothers and sisters in Christ is that they will pick up some of the weight of your cares.

> *"Carry each other's burdens, and in this way*
> *you will fulfill the law of Christ."*
>
> — Galatians 6:2

Just as exercise and fitness training ensure you have the stamina and strength to endure a physical assault, cultivating relationships with fellow believers who understand the unique issues you face on the job is an imperative preventive measure. Regardless of how tough you are, you will find yourself carrying an overwhelming burden at some point in your first responder career. This is a career field in which an undue amount of stress is regularly placed upon you. As a Christian first responder, you are put under even more pressure, for you are aware of the source of all the horrible things to which you are exposed. But here is the hope: God is in control.

> *"Let us not become weary in doing good, for*
> *at the proper time we will reap a harvest*
> *if we do not give up. Therefore, as we*
> *have opportunity, let us do good to all*

> *people, especially to those who belong to*
> *the family of believers."*

— GALATIANS 6: 9-10

Your unsaved coworkers do not have this hope or the peace it brings.

Treating fellow believers in this manner is expected of us as Christians and does not merit any special reward.

> *"If you love those who love you, what reward*
> *will you get? Are not even the tax*
> *collectors doing that? And if you greet*
> *only your own people, what are you doing*
> *more than others? Do not even pagans do*
> *that?"*

— MATTHEW 5:46-47

What would it look like if you were able to start doing this for those who hate you simply for the uniform you wear and the authority you represent? Can you imagine the potential impact that Christ could have through you if you submitted to this in your daily life?

What would be a legitimate reason that you would even want to treat your enemies in this way? After all, isn't it dangerous to be too friendly to these 'sheep in wolves clothing'? Absolutely! It is extremely dangerous to let your guard down around these violent predators. This is not the point being made, and I would be remiss to suggest that this is the intention of scripture, especially in regard to first responders. In Matthew 10:16, Jesus said, *"I am sending you out like sheep among wolves. Therefore be as shrewd as snakes and as innocent as doves.*" Christ knew the dangers of being overly naive in such a dangerous and fallen world. The intent for the point being made here is found in 1 Peter 2:15, "*For it is God's will that by doing good you should silence the ignorant talk of foolish people.*" Remember, being able to walk this tightrope is in order to bring about God's glory while still being able to keep these deviants from getting the upper hand.

> *"But in your hearts revere Christ as Lord.*
> *Always be prepared to give an answer to*
> *everyone who asks you to give the reason*
> *for the hope that you have. But do this*
> *with gentleness and respect, 16. keeping a*
> *clear conscience, so that those who speak*
> *maliciously against your good behavior*
> *in Christ may be ashamed of their*
> *slander."*
>
> — 1 Peter 3:15-16

It is for your protection and benefit to start treating those over whom you have authority in this manner. Christ wants to ensure that you do not stumble or fall victim to their schemes.

A Transcending Peace

How do you even get to a place in your faith that allows you to treat these people in the way you are called? There is absolutely zero chance that you could ever meet this achievement through your own power and strength.

> *"And the peace of God, which transcends all*
> *understanding, will guard your hearts*
> *and your minds in Christ Jesus."*

— Philippians 4:7

Ultimately, you must rely on the Lord to give you the tools you will need to achieve the level of the psalmist outlined in chapter 119 in order to make a spiritual impact. Scripture, prayer, and fellowship with other believers (whether they are first responders or not) are the tools that are readily available to you and at your disposal to be used in your pursuit of making this impact.

Meditation is another great tool in your arsenal.

> *"Finally, brothers and sisters, whatever is*
> *true, whatever is noble, whatever is right,*
> *whatever is pure, whatever is lovely,*
> *whatever is admirable—if anything is*
> *excellent or praiseworthy—think about*
> *such things. 9. Whatever you have*
> *learned or received or heard from me, or*
> *seen in me—put it into practice. And the*
> *God of peace will be with you."*

— Philippians 4:8-9

Purposefully directing your thoughts towards these things is one of the greatest force multipliers in relation to your spiritual warfare.

Like any other skill that enhances your ability to be an effective first responder, spiritual meditation takes a tremendous amount of discipline to perform on a continuous basis. Similar to how it takes the performance thousands of repetitions of a particular skill in order for you to perform it under stress, so too is spiritual meditation. How often do you find your mind drifting while in prayer? If you are anything like me, the answer is ALL THE TIME. Can you empathize with the disciples falling asleep in the garden when Jesus went off to pray for an hour? It is difficult to pray for an hour, let alone without ceasing. The more I think I understand the spiritual warfare raging around me the more I realize how little I know. But I totally understand why they fell asleep. The reason you try to pray like this, though, is to show your obedience to Jesus. Not for your glory, but for Christ's.

> *"Do your best to present yourself to God as*
> *one approved, a worker who does not*
> *need to be ashamed and who correctly*
> *handles the word of truth."*
>
> — 2 Timothy 2:15

Remember, the goal is progress, not perfection.

Patience is another tool we have at our disposal to help us make an impact within our sphere of influence. Every single military veteran has had patience ingrained into the very fiber of their being. The 'hurry up and wait' lifestyle prevalent in every branch of the armed forces has given you the coping mechanisms needed to deal with extremely frustrating situations. For those of us who served prior to the extensive use of the internet, cellular devices, tablets, and computers, your coping skills are light years ahead of those who are reliant on these devices. As Christians, we are called to have a patient disposition.

> *"Be patient, then, brothers and sisters, until*
> *the Lord's coming. See how the farmer*
> *waits for the land to yield its valuable*
> *crop, patiently waiting for the autumn*
> *and spring rains.*
> *8. You too, be patient and stand firm, because*
> *the Lord's coming is near."*

— JAMES 5:7-8

If at all possible, seek to develop your patience through a conscientious and organic way. Patience and forgiveness are probably two of the most highly contentious virtues you can ask for in prayer. Ask anyone who has ever prayed for either of these and you will learn that you will get everything asked for and then some.

> *"No temptation has overtaken you except*
> *what is common to mankind. And God*
> *is faithful; he will not let you be tempted*
> *beyond what you can bear. But when you*
> *are tempted, he will also provide a way*
> *out so that you can endure it."*

— 1 CORINTHIANS 10:13

You will not be given more than you can handle, but you will be given more than you want. You will be the better for it, but you will be hard-pressed to find a rougher road upon which you will have traveled.

Making an impact within your family, circle of friends, workplace, and community is a natural consequence of intentionally seeking to do God's will in your life. Treating those people with whom you come in contact on a regular basis will result in rich blessings. This will be accomplished through you when you follow Christ's example.

> *"Do everything without grumbling or*
>   *arguing,*
> 15. *so that you may become blameless and*
>   *pure, 'children of God without fault in a*
>   *warped and crooked generation.' Then*
>   *you will shine among them like stars in*
>   *the sky*
> 16. *as you hold firmly to the word of life.*
>   *And then I will be able to boast on the*
>   *day of Christ that I did not run or labor*
>   *in vain."*
>
> — Philippians 2: 14-16

Imagine the impact you can see within your family, friends, and coworkers if you were to follow just this one command. Would your spouse be dumbfounded if you started doing those small tasks around the house without arguing or complaining? What about your supervisor? What would your friends think if you stopped grumbling? Every single one of them would think you were kidnapped by aliens and replaced with a clone!

But seriously, the impact you can have on your direct sphere of influence can be massive. The key to making such an impact is to take small, intentional, and incremental steps to follow the examples set forth in scripture. Philippians 3:13-14 says, *"Brothers and sisters, I do not consider myself yet to have taken hold of it. But one thing I do: Forgetting what is behind and straining toward what is ahead, 14. I press on toward the goal to win the prize for which God has called me heavenward in Christ Jesus.*" Paul understood the difficulty in the path. He makes it clear that the goal is progress over perfection. One is measurable and attainable. The other is an impossibility.

CONFIDENCE IN CHRIST ALONE

We strive to follow biblical examples because it is not our strength that makes this impact.

> "being confident of this, that he who began
> a good work in you will carry it on to
> completion until the day of Christ
> Jesus."

> — PHILIPPIANS 1:6

Jesus works out the impact He wants to achieve. He effectively uses us in the manner which suits Him best. Your influence in helping to bring about this impact can be a one-time thing, like when you simply sow the seed. God will water it and tend it to maturity.

Or you can have an ongoing influence in which Christ directly uses you many times over the course of several years, reaping the harvest at the appointed hour. Jesus said in John 10:28-29: "*I give them eternal life, and they shall never perish; no one will snatch them out of my hand. 29. My Father, who has given them to me, is greater than all; no one can snatch them out of my Father's hand.*" You have a real opportunity to be a shepherd to a lost sheep. What more of an impact would you want than that?

What motivates you to make this impact? Does God

care about our behaviors? Does He care about how we speak, or what our thought life entails? Of course. Does He care more about these outward expressions of our religion, or do the motivations behind the behaviors matter to Him more? You know the answer. God's primary concern is for your heart and the outward expression of your submission to His will in an effort to please Him.

CHALLENGE COIN:

- Identify one person from three different parts of your life* and commit to praying for them at least once daily for thirty days. i.e., one family member, one coworker, and one 'frequent flyer.'
- Identify at least one area in your life that you can replace with intentional spiritual meditation. Build this up to at least thirty minutes per day.
- Commit to fellowship with at least two other believers within your circle of friends at least one time each week. Understand that it is preferable this fellowship occurs in person; however, it is an acceptable alternative if the only way this fellowship can occur is online, via text, or over the phone.

Chapter Seven
Retirement

"Do not cast me away when I am old; do
not forsake me when my strength is
gone."

— Psalm 71:9

When I was younger, I did not seriously consider preparing for retirement. After all, in my youth, I was firmly to be found within Proverbs 20:29, *"The glory of young men is their strength, gray hair the splendor of the old."* I started my career as a United States Navy Corpsman, deploying to the Persian Gulf and Somalia with the United States Marine Corps. I did not just glory in my own strength; I reveled in it. It was a continual source of pride to outperform my Marine brothers in push-ups, sit-ups, and (yes) pull-ups.

I was utterly and completely assured of my worthiness based on the skills and abilities flowing from within myself. It was several years and more than a few bad choices later before Christ plucked me from the mire, dusted me off, and knocked some sense into my thick skull. I am now striving to live out Proverbs 16:31, *"Gray hair is a crown of splendor; it is attained in the way of righteousness."* I am learning that each one of these gray hairs represents a lesson learned, an obstacle that has been overcome, or a heartache for which I am the better for having endured. I am now excitedly looking forward to the day after the day I retire.

> *"Have I not commanded you? Be strong and*
> *courageous. Do not be afraid; do not be*
> *discouraged, for the Lord your God will*
> *be with you wherever you go."*
>
> — JOSHUA 1:9

What I did not consider when I was younger was the fact that it is more than possible to continue making an impact once your active involvement as a first responder has ended. It is a fact for many that retirement has become the perfect opportunity to increase the impact they have on those still serving in the first responder community. While other first responders spend their newly found free time on the golf course, in the wood shop, or traveling, many Christian first responders have chosen to continue to serve. These retirees have just found a new outlet for their deeply ingrained desire to help.

Do not take this the wrong way. There is absolutely nothing wrong in pursuing your hobbies and passions in retirement. Spending time with your grandchildren, traveling the world and enjoying God's wonderful gift of nature, or engaging in a simply pleasurable activity holds every bit as much honor as anything else you can pursue in retirement. Once you have reached this stage in your life, you have definitely earned the right to spend your time in any way you see fit. Anything that you choose to pursue in retirement, short of parking yourself on the couch for an uninterrupted month-long Magnum P.I. marathon can be used to further your impact.

Post-Retirement Ministry

Many theologians claim that the only proper activity in retirement for a Christian is ministerial service. It is widely regarded in these circles that as you retire and no longer need an income from the ministry, you are obligated as a Christian to perform such ministerial duties. I see this for what it is: purely legalistic hogwash. You are free to pursue whatever you deem fit in retirement.

And do not let me, your pastor, a revered televangelist, or any other person make you feel that how you choose to spend your retirement years is any less important than volunteering your time in the ministry. Now, let's stop kicking that dead horse and look at what the bible has to say about what kind of impact you can make in retirement.

First of all, retirement is a biblically mandated progression of life.

> *"but at the age of fifty, they must retire from their regular service and work no longer."*

> — Numbers 8:25

Although this age mandate was designated for Levites serving in the temple, the time will come when you will be required to stop working. Regardless of whether you are eagerly anticipating this life transition or dreading it, retirement is an ordinance of God. He designed our bodies to deteriorate as we age, resulting in our being less able to perform certain functions as time goes on. This is simply a fact of life.

Exercise, proper diet, and personal interactions with an engaging support structure have all been shown to slow the aging process. But, the inevitable truth is you will not be able to perform the same amount or type of work at the same level of competence as you age. This is especially true for the type of work you perform as a first responder. Backs go bad, knees get tricky, and necks get kinked all too often in this line of work. And this career field demands an incredibly high price from your body over the years, let alone the decades.

This physical decline, however slight it might be, will eventually lead to your being a liability within the first responder community. This does not mean that you are no longer of any fundamental value to your organization. Nor does this mean you suddenly find you are lacking in any quantifiable skills. It just means you will have to find a new outlet for all the valuable skills you have developed over the decades. Your desire to be of service does not arbitrarily go away the morning after you retire.

A USEFUL PURPOSE REMAINS

God was aware that you would still want to do something in the period of time between full employment and when you are no longer able to work. God even told Moses this desire to continue working was not only proper but acceptable in Numbers 8:26, "*They may assist their brothers in performing their duties at the tent of meeting, but they themselves must not do the work.*" Now, as understandable as it is to have this desire to continue to serve others, how that service manifests itself is one hundred percent your call. We will not start kicking that dead horse again.

Regardless of what you choose to pursue in retirement as a Christian first responder, your end goal will look far different than your unsaved coworkers, as we read in Matthew 6:19-20,

> *"'Do not store up for yourselves treasures on earth, where moths and vermin destroy, and where thieves break in and steal. 20. But store up for yourselves treasures in heaven, where moths and vermin do not destroy, and where thieves do not break in and steal.'"*

Your true treasure is not in this world but in the one to come. A word of caution here. This does not mean you are free from your obligations to prepare to support yourself in retirement.

As a first responder, you are a responsible citizen of your community. As a Christian, you are called to be a good steward of the gifts that have been bestowed upon you. These are two sides of the same coin and are not necessarily opposing viewpoints. It is within a person's approach to money where the contradictory ideologies reside, referenced in 1 Timothy 6:9-10,

> *"Those who want to get rich fall into temptation and a trap and into many foolish and harmful desires that plunge people into ruin and destruction. 10. For*

> *the love of money is a root of all kinds of*
> *evil. Some people, eager for money, have*
> *wandered from the faith and pierced*
> *themselves with many griefs."*

This is a matter of mindset. Similar to how the fifth commandment was changed in an effort to elicit a moralistic belief, a small part of this passage has been warped to bring about a legalist mandate. Money, in and of itself, is amoral. It has been intentionally misrepresented to instill a sense that money has an immoral quality. This is simply not a biblical truth. It is when you are willing to trade your principles in exchange for money when trouble ensues. How many times did you witness someone's progressive moral decline during your career, ultimately leading to that person's disgrace? It is why greed has been listed among the seven deadly sins.

The Balance Between Need and Greed

Ensuring you can provide for your expenses through the duration of your life, regardless of how long that may be, is solid biblical teaching as stated in 1 Timothy 5:8,

> *"Anyone who does not provide for their*
> *relatives, and especially for their own*
> *household, has denied the faith and is*
> *worse than an unbeliever."*

Another way to look at how we should regard money in retirement is found in Proverbs 13:22, *"A good person leaves an inheritance for their children's children, but a sinner's wealth is stored up for the righteous."*

While there is always a temptation to want more, you are solidly within sound biblical principles if you find your approach to money with the attitude that it is not yours to keep. This mindset will ease the burden of learning to live on less than what you were making as a full-time first responder.

As you navigate the new normal that is retirement, new routines will develop organically. Within the cycles of these new routines is where you will find what it is that makes you thrive. It is not uncommon for you to have found your self-worth in what you do as a first responder. As a Christian, the truth of your self-worth is found in Christ. But you know as well as I do that it is hard to separate yourself from what you do. This does not change once you hang up the uniform.

Maybe this self-worth conundrum is the reason why so many first responders go back to school and get some variation of theology degree. How many retired first responders do you know personally who have become pastors, therapists, counselors, or biblical teachers? Again, there is nothing wrong with scholarly pursuits in this curriculum, as long as your self-worth remains in Christ and not your newfound erudition or position.

> *"Even to your old age and gray hairs I am he,*
> *I am he who will sustain you. I have*
> *made you and I will carry you; I will*
> *sustain you and I will rescue you."*
>
> — Isaiah 46:4

It is Christ who sustains you, now and forever.

Retirement is not something for you to dread. Embrace

the ever-diminishing gap between here and there. If you have already reached 'there,' enjoy every moment God grants you in this season. After all, not everyone makes it that far.

Number Your Days

A police officer can expect to live to 57 years old, correctional officers to 59, and each can plan on a mere five years in retirement, on average. That is nearly 22 years less than the average adult life expectancy. Firefighters can expect to live 12.5 years less than the average adult. In contrast, medical personnel fare far better, with 39% of doctors and nurses living longer than the national average. While these statistics may be distressing, what are you to do? We are instructed not to worry in Matthew 6:27, *"Can any one of you by worrying add a single hour to your life?"*

Diet, exercise, and recreation will play a significant role in mitigating the negative effects this career has on your body, but even so, the very days of your life have already been numbered, as read in Psalm 139:16, *"Your eyes saw my unformed body; all the days ordained for me were written in your book before one of them came to be."* These healthy habits ensure you have a good quality of life. They do not necessarily ensure you have a good quantity of life.

Do not let this be a source of disquiet in your retirement years. After all, the older you get, the more you should long for your time with Jesus. When you were young, it was natural to feel like you would live forever.

This is a natural design process of your brain development. As the years roll by in your post-retirement life, you will be drawn to accepting the truth of this certainty. As a Christian, the goal is to meet Jesus and tell

Him what Paul wrote in 2 Timothy 4:7, *"I have fought the good fight, I have finished the race, I have kept the faith."* And when you hear the words from Matthew 25:21, *"Well done, good and faithful servant!"*, you will not go forward full of fear and downcast in spirit, but with unmitigated joy.

If you truly know this is to be the response you will receive upon your death, what do you have to fear or regret?

Challenge Coin:

- As much as you can, commit to mentoring a younger Christian first responder within your community. You can determine the most appropriate course to ensure that you pass along your knowledge, both professionally and spiritually, to this younger generation.
- As much as you can, commit to intentional prayer for three first responders within your community. This prayer should be daily and in addition to your other prayer life.
- As much as you can, volunteer for one position for which you have always had a desire but for which you did not have the time, i.e., usher, youth leader, coach, or elder. This can be within or separate from your local church.

Notes

1. Chapter One

1. Merriam-Webster.com Dictionary, s.v. "worship," accessed May 15, 2024, https://www.merriam-webster.com/dictionary/worship.

About the Author

John Jones is a former US Navy Fleet Marine Force (FMF) Hospital Corpsman where he experienced combat when deployed to Somalia in 1995. He has also been a Corrections Officer, Deputy Sheriff, and most recently retiring as a Senior Federal Law Enforcement Officer. John holds a BS in Criminal Justice Administration, and a MS in Security Management from Bellevue University. Mr. Jones has obtained both state and federal LEO credentials and holds several federal instructor certifications. Mr. Jones is the co-author of the undergraduate textbook entitled: ***The Fundamentals of Security Management: A Common Sense Approach***.